Evaluating Police Tactics

Evaluating Police Tactics

An Empirical Assessment of Room Entry Techniques

J. Pete Blair
M. Hunter Martaindale

Routledge
Taylor & Francis Group

LONDON AND NEW YORK

First published 2014 by Anderson Publishing

Published 2015 by Routledge
2 Park Square, Milton Park, Abingdon, Oxon OX14 4RN

and by Routledge
711 Third Avenue, New York, NY 10017, USA

Routledge is an imprint of the Taylor & Francis Group, an informa business

British Library Cataloguing-in-Publication Data
A catalogue record for this book is available from the British Library

Library of Congress Cataloging-in-Publication Data
A catalog record for this book is available from the Library of Congress

ISBN 978-0-323-28066-2 (pbk)

Printed and bound in the United States of America by
Edwards Brothers Malloy on sustainably sourced paper

To those who are willing place themselves in harm's way to protect the rest of us.

ABOUT THE AUTHORS

J. Pete Blair is an Associate Professor of Criminal Justice at Texas State University. He is also the Director of Research for the Advanced Law Enforcement Rapid Response Training (ALERRT) center at Texas State. Dr. Blair has published research on a variety of police-related topics including a book about active shooter events and response. He has also presented his research on active shooter events and police tactics to diverse audiences across the country including the Police Executive Research Forum (PERF), Federal Bureau of Investigation (FBI), and Texas Association of School Boards (TASB).

M. Hunter Martaindale is a Ph.D. student at Texas State University – School of Criminal Justice. Hunter works as a research assistant for both the Advanced Law Enforcement Rapid Response Training (ALERRT) program and the Texas School Safety Center. His current research projects involve active shooter analysis and improving law enforcement tactics and efficiency.

CONTENTS

ACKNOWLEDGMENTS

This project would not have been possible without the help of a great many people. First, we would like to thank all of the ALERRT staff for their guidance and help. More specifically, Don Montague approved our plans and gave us ALERRT's full support. David Burns, Terry Nichols, and John Curnutt provided us with an enormous amount of tactical insight and experience in addition to playing key roles in many of the experiments. Zane Childress and Randall Watkins provided (nearly) perfect logistical assistance and also played key roles in conducting the experiments. We are also grateful to the many ALERRT graduate assistants who lugged gear around and were constantly shot up in the name of science. We are indebted to the many law enforcement officers who took time out of their lives to participate in the experiments and provide their insights to us. Paul Howe's vast experience and tactical wisdom were invaluable.

To all those that helped make this project a success, we hope the knowledge generated makes your life a little safer.

Whether responding to a burglar alarm or clearing a building after discovering an open door, patrol officers routinely conduct room entries (moving from one location in the building to another) as a part of their duties. Generally, there is no one in the structure at the time of the search, but in the few cases when a hostile suspect is present, the risk of injury to the officer is high. Additionally, since the mass shooting at Columbine, we have expected patrol officers to enter buildings where active shooting is occurring, find the shooter, and stop the killing. This is clearly a very dangerous situation as the suspect has already demonstrated a willingness to commit murder.

Since Columbine, a number of private and public groups have offered active shooter training to patrol officers. A component of this training involves teaching officers how to conduct room entries when there may be a hostile suspect inside. Different training groups teach a variety of entry styles and techniques. For years, a debate has raged around the pros and cons of the different styles and techniques. Advocates and detractors of the styles and techniques have generally relied upon their authority and personal experiences to support their cases. What is lacking in this area is solid empirical data to support the development of evidence-based best practices. This book seeks to provide these data.

We present detailed literature reviews to connect existing scientific research to the issue of room entries. We then present a series of five experiments to test the beliefs that we developed based upon the literature. Founded upon these experiments and the existing literature, we believe that the hasty slice style, combined with the hybrid entry technique, produces the best officer performance during a room entry and should be adopted as best practices for active shooter training. Even for those who disagree, we hope that the data provided here will be useful in informing policy and procedure.

We are extremely pleased to present this work as one of the first offerings for the Real World Criminology Series. Pete Blair and Hunter Martaindale's description of a series of experiments on police tactics conducted at the Advanced Law Enforcement Rapid Response Training (ALERRT) Center at Texas State University is exactly the type of work we had in mind when developing this series. Our goal was to bridge the divide between academics and field professionals by presenting research and/or program evaluations in all areas of criminal justice in a manner that was easily accessible to everyone, both in terms of marketing and in the manner of presentation. The efforts described in this monograph offer a perfect example of how an academic/scientific approach can improve the field, in this case by making tactics safer for law enforcement professionals. Through a wide dissemination of these findings, others can build on the knowledge offered here.

"Evidence-based practices" is a phrase that is probably overused and given more lip service than rigid adherence in the field today; however, this monograph offers one example of how law enforcement practices can be evaluated in a more careful and scientific way to determine the most efficacious techniques. In this case, room entry method was the issue, but the approach of reviewing relevant literature and then developing experiments that utilize available technology and statistical analysis to determine findings is a model that can be applied to a wide range of law enforcement practices. As with all research, the work described here raises additional questions, but the findings should be of great interest to law enforcement practitioners and trainers. Further, the findings may also be of interest to academics interested in a variety of topical areas as disparate as the use of deadly force and perceptual distortions. We hope the reader will benefit from the findings in this monograph and look for other monographs in the series that may be of interest.

−*Joycelyn M. Pollock*

CHAPTER *1*

Introduction

On May 3, 2010, Police Officer Brian Huff responded to a report of shots fired at a vacant home in Detroit, Michigan, at approximately 3:30 am (ODMP, 2010). Officer Huff entered the residence with several other officers. Upon entry, a gunman opened fire. Officer Huff was fatally wounded and four other officers received non-life-threatening injuries. The suspect was wounded in a barrage of return gunfire. This is an example of a situation when officers executed a room entry (moving from one location within a structure to another) and were injured by a hostile gunman.

While officers being killed or wounded when performing a room entry is uncommon, room entries themselves are not. For example, officers must frequently search buildings when they receive alarm calls or discover an open door. When these searches are conducted, there is always a possibility that the searching officers will encounter a hostile suspect.

Additionally, since the mass shooting at Columbine, we have expected patrol officers to enter buildings where a suspect is shooting people, confront the attacker, and stop the killing (Blair et al., 2013). This means that we expect patrol officers to perform room entries against suspects who have already demonstrated a willingness to kill. This is obviously an extremely dangerous situation. Training in how to handle active shooter events has been provided by a variety of public and private entities, and these training groups teach officers a variety of room entry techniques.

Despite the frequency and potential danger inherent in conducting room entries, very little empirical research has explored the effectiveness of the different entry styles and techniques. This book details a series of experiments designed to explore the efficacy of two general entry styles and three specific entry tactics. Because patrol officers across the country are receiving this training in relationship to active shooter events, we have focused our research on what styles and techniques are effective for patrol officers. It is our hope that the information contained here will provide practitioners and trainers with solid empirical data that can be used to inform best practices.

We begin with a general argument for the empirical testing of police tactics. In the following chapters, we detail the two general entry styles and present an experiment designed to test the efficacy of the styles. Following that, we discuss three commonly used entry techniques and present a series of experiments that were conducted to address the effectiveness of these techniques.

1.1 WHY CONDUCT EMPIRICAL RESEARCH INTO POLICE TACTICS?

When the first author began his graduate studies in policing, he was consistently surprised by the almost complete lack of rigorous empirical validation (i.e., scientific research) relating to police tactics. He had assumed that police tactics had been well studied; yet, time and time again, he found that validation was lacking despite frequent calls for criminal justice policy and procedures to be rooted in science (Sherman, 1998; Sherman, Farrington, Welsh, & Mackenzie, 2002; Weisburd et al., 2005). Some areas of police practice have, of course, received attention (e.g., routine patrol, hot spots policing, eyewitness identification, and interviewing), but many areas of police practice remain largely untouched.

This means that policing tactics have largely been developed from knowledge sources other than empirical research. These sources likely include a combination of intuition, personal experience, tradition, and authority.

Each of these sources can provide valid knowledge (i.e., knowledge that reflects the actual state of the world), but each can also produce incorrect knowledge (i.e., knowledge that does not reflect the actual state of the world). For example, the prevalence of confirmatory bias has been well documented in the psychological literature (Kahneman, 2011). Confirmatory bias refers to the process of information seeking whereby individuals who hold an opinion on some issue only seek out information that supports that opinion and ignore information that refutes the position. The result of this bias is that personal experience may produce knowledge that is not valid. For example, if there is a room entry technique that I think works, I will only pay attention to times when the technique worked and ignore the times when it did not.

It can also be useful to divide knowledge into two broad categories: explicit knowledge, which has been developed from, and subjected to, rigorous empirical testing (i.e., the scientific method); and implicit knowledge, which has developed naturally and organically without being exposed to rigorous empirical testing (i.e., not scientifically validated).

Much of the knowledge that we utilize in everyday life is implicit, and this implicit knowledge is often accurate because personal experiences, tradition, and authority often produce correct beliefs. For example, I drive the same way to work almost every day because, based upon my implicit understanding of roads, traffic, and vehicles, I believe it to be the fastest way to get to work. I have not driven all of the possible alternate routes in a repeated and systematic manner to empirically confirm this belief (i.e., make it explicit knowledge). Yet, on the few occasions when I have been forced to take an alternate route—due to a traffic accident, for example—I have found that these other routes are indeed slower. My implicit knowledge, then, appears to be correct.

However, implicit knowledge is not always correct. Kahneman and Klien (2009) have conducted extensive research into decision making and have identified two conditions that are necessary in order for people to develop correct implicit (i.e., intuitive) beliefs. The first is that there must be cues in the environment that provide accurate information about the actual state of things. That is, the environment must be consistent enough for people to be able to make accurate judgments. Making an accurate determination regarding which route is quickest to drive provides many reliable cues. For example, highways will generally be faster than surface streets because highway speed limits are higher and there are no stoplights or stop signs. Being a highway, however, is not a perfect indicator, as there may sometimes be an accident on the highway that makes it slower than the surface street. What is important is that highways are usually faster. If there were frequent accidents on the highway such that it was not usually faster, then highways would not be a reliable indicator for the quickness of a trip.

The second requirement is that people must have opportunities to learn what the relevant cues are (Kahneman & Klien, 2009). Key to this learning is feedback; that is, the person makes judgments and receives information about whether or not those judgments were correct. When it comes to choosing correct routes for quickest travel, most of us have had a lifetime of feedback regarding our decisions (particularly in our local contexts). We choose a route, make the journey, and know how long it took us to get to our destination. Given that driving has reliable cues in the environment and drivers have ample opportunity to learn these cues, it is likely that our implicit knowledge about the quickest routes will be generally accurate.

To illustrate implicit knowledge in the policing context, we will present two examples—one where the implicit knowledge was falsified through empirical testing and one where the implicit knowledge was validated through empirical testing. We will start with the example in which implicit knowledge proved to be incorrect.

In December 1991, a house fire in Corsicana, Texas, claimed the lives of three children. At the time of the fire, the mother was shopping for Christmas presents. The father, Cameron Todd Willingham, claimed he was asleep when his young daughter awoke him. She told him the house was on fire. He claimed he told her to get out of the house while he tried to rescue his one-year-old twin daughters. He further claimed that he entered the girls' bedroom but could not find them due to the smoke. He suffered burns and then escaped. Neighbors and first responders testified he was extremely distraught while outside the residence. Willingham was charged with, and subsequently found guilty of, the murder of his children.

The fire marshal presented the opinion that ultimately led to the conviction of Willingham. This opinion was based upon physical markings found at the scene and the marshal's implicit understanding of these markings. There were char patterns in the shape of puddles, multiple starting points, crazed glass (i.e., spider web-like markings in glass), and other evidence that suggested the fire was both fast and hot. This information, according to the marshal (and consistent with the implicit beliefs of many arson investigators at the time), pointed to a liquid accelerant (such as starter fluid) and arson; but research has found that these things also happen when a flashover occurs. A flashover happens when most of the combustible materials in a room reach ignition point at the same time and burst into flame simultaneously. Indeed, many who have reviewed the Willingham case believe that it was caused by a flashover (Beyler, 2009).

Willingham was executed in February of 2004. The execution went through even though experts had rebuked many of the initial findings. Willingham has since received a posthumous pardon.

Cases such as this have led to a push to explicitly examine the foundations of many areas of forensic science. The National Academy of Sciences (NAS), under Congressional direction, established a committee in 2006 to examine the forensic sciences, disseminate best practices, and develop recommendations. The overarching goal of this effort was to examine whether or not various areas of forensic science were actually based in science (i.e., explicit knowledge). The forensic science disciplines that were examined included, but were not limited to, biological evidence, toolmark and firearms identification, bloodstain pattern analysis, and the analysis of hair and fiber evidence. With the exception of nuclear DNA analysis, none of the forensic science areas were found to meet the standards required to be called scientific. This surprising finding has led to vast efforts to conduct the research needed to validate and, where needed, improve the scientific basis upon which these techniques are based.

While implicit knowledge may be invalidated when scientifically challenged (e.g., the Willingham case), this is not always the case. A strong criminological example when implicit knowledge was correct and validated can be found in hot spots policing. The term "hot spots" was coined (in criminological literature) when research revealed that crime was spatially concentrated in small areas rather than evenly distributed (Pierce, Spaar, & Briggs, 1988; Weiburd, Maher, & Sherman, 1992). In fact, research found that over half of all urban crime is committed in a few spatial locations (Sherman, Gartin, & Buerger, 1989).

While this finding was fairly new to researchers, police had long believed spatial factors were important to crime problems and that focusing their efforts in these hot spots (called hot spots policing) could reduce crime (Bittner, 1970). Critics, however, argued that these focused efforts would have little impact on crime rates and may simply move crime around to new areas (referred to as displacement; Reppetto, 1976).

Over the decades, numerous studies had been conducted to examine these beliefs. In 2012, Braga, Papachristos, and Hureau published a quantitative summary of these studies (called a meta-analysis). Braga et al. identified 19 studies. Overall, they found that hot spots policing reduced crime and did not displace it to other areas. In fact, their findings suggested that hot spots policing may actually reduce crime in the surrounding areas (called a diffusion of benefits). This is a clear case when the implicit beliefs of the police were validated by empirical research.

While research sometimes validates implicit knowledge, this may not be the case when it comes to conducting tactical room entries. Recall that in order for implicit knowledge to produce correct beliefs, there must be both reliable cues in the environment and the opportunity to learn those cues. We believe that there are sufficiently reliable cues or processes to allow accurate implicit knowledge to develop in the case of room entries. Research into reaction times (which will be discussed later) shows that people exhibit very consistent reaction times to stimuli in similar situations, for example (Blair, Pollock, Montague, Nichols, Curnutt, & Burns, 2011; Lewinski & Hudson, 2003). The ways in which people move, and the time it takes to complete these movements, are also fairly regular. The effects of threats on one's ability to maintain situational awareness are also reliable (Grossman & Christensen, 2008).

However, we believe that there is a problem with accurate feedback when it comes to room entries. For patrol officers conducting building searches, there will often be no suspect in the building; therefore, the officers do not receive accurate feedback regarding the effectiveness of their entries. Any entry appears to be tactically effective when no one is present.

In the vast majority of cases when a suspect is in the building during a search, the suspect is not hostile and will not attempt to fight the officer. Again, it does not matter what entry the officer performs when a suspect does not choose to fight because the officer will not be injured and the suspect will be adequately dealt with. What the officers did may have been completely tactically unsound, but because no one was hurt, they receive incorrect feedback about the tactics that were utilized.

The only event that provides accurate information about the tactics used during a room entry, then, is one in which the suspect actively fights (i.e., shoots at) the officers. These are rare events. In 2011, 63 officers were killed with firearms and 2,208 were assaulted with fire-arms. About 10% of the officers assaulted with firearms were injured (FBI, 2011). This gives a rough estimate of 2,300 firearms assaults in the sample of roughly 540,000 officers whose agencies provided data. This means that approximately 0.4% of officers were assaulted with firearms in 2011. Additionally, many, if not most, of these assaults did not involve room entries. These statistics show that the opportunity for feedback about room entries for individual officers is extremely lim-ited. Of course, feedback could be obtained through realistic force-on-force training exercises in which officers and role-player suspects engage in simulated gun battles, but many agencies do not engage in this type of training and the lessons learned may be inaccurate, as dis-cussed later.

Tactical (SWAT) teams are perhaps in the best position to receive feedback on the effectiveness of their room entries because they are often tasked with taking high-risk suspects into custody and often do this by raiding houses. But, again, the vast majority of the suspects that SWAT teams encounter do not attempt to actively fight the team. While some of the suspects may be deterred or prevented from fighting by the surprise, speed, and controlled aggression of the SWAT team entry, many simply would not fight armed police no matter what type of entry was done. So here, again, is a feedback problem.

More generally, the lack of feedback applies to all higher-level use of force situations for officers. While officers are trained in how to properly utilize force, the need for more serious levels of force is rare. For example, the Bureau of Justice Statistics conducted the 2008 Police-Public Contact Survey as a supplement to the National Crime Victimization Survey. An estimated 1.4% of those surveyed had force used or threatened during their most recent contact with law enforce-ment (BJS, 2008). In a related study, Hickman, Piquero, and Garner (2008) found that 1.5% of police-citizen contacts resulted in either the use of force or the threat of force. Of these cases, only a very small percentage (0.2%) of police-citizen encounters resulted in lethal force (i.e., use of a firearm) being applied or threatened. Geller and Scott (1992) determined that the average officer would have to work 1,299 years in Milwaukee, 694 years in New York City, or 198 years in Dallas to be statistically expected to shoot and kill a suspect.

Additionally, it is not always clear that when an officer is shot at, she or he learns from that event. For example, one SWAT team conducted a raid on a house during which several of the team members were shot. Since the event, the team has given several briefings to other officers in the area. These briefings focus on the importance of the downed officer drills that the team had extensively practiced but do not question the decision to conduct the raid or the tactics used to make entry, despite several team members being seriously wounded.

The point is that implicit knowledge may be wrong, and explicit knowledge testing (i.e., the scientific method) is critical. The use of the scientific method allows us to systematically test the different entry styles and techniques in an attempt to assess the strengths and weaknesses of the techniques while eliminating or controlling for many of the problems that arise with implicit methods of knowledge creation. Next, we discuss the two most well-known styles of entry: the "dump" and the "slice" styles of entry.

CHAPTER 2

Room Entry Styles

There are two dominant room entry styles taught to law enforcement officers. The primary difference between the two styles involves what happens before the officers on the entry team cross the threshold of the door into the room. We refer to the first style as the "dump" and the second as the "slice."

2.1 THE DUMP

If you have seen a police SWAT team doing a room entry in the movies, you have probably seen the dump in action. This style of entry is sometimes called a dynamic entry or a fill and flow style of entry and has been used by SWAT teams for some time (Blair, Nichols, Burns, & Curnutt, 2013). The officers in the entry team generally approach the doorway to the room they are entering in a singlefile line called a stack. The first person in the stack goes directly in to the room and the rest of the officers follow. Officers are supposed to alternate the direction that they go when they enter the room in order to make certain that all of the threat areas of the room are covered. In Figure 2.1, the first officer in the stack went straight into the room. The second officer then will take a 90-degree turn to the right. The third officer will fill in to the right of the first officer and the fourth officer will fill in to the left of the second officer. How far the officers move into the room will vary based upon the setup of the room and the preferences of the team. Some teams like the officers to move all the way to the corner of a room and some like the officers to move about a third of the way between the door and the corner. What is important is that the officers move in far enough so that they are clear of the doorway (which is often referred to as the "fatal funnel") and the other officers in the team can get into the room.

The shaded wedges in Figure 2.1 represent the primary areas of responsibility for each officer. After each officer ensures that his or her primary area is clear, the officer then checks the other areas to make certain that these areas are also clear. In the event that the first officer to

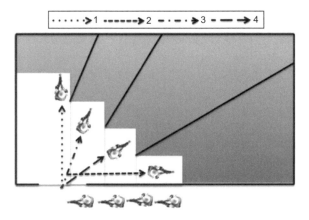

Figure 2.1 Dump movement. Wedges indicate the officers' areas of primary responsibility.

enter encounters an armed threat and engages in a gunfight, the following officers are still supposed to first clear their primary threat areas and then engage the suspect. This is to ensure that all threats in the room are addressed instead of just focusing on the first one to appear.

When active shooter programs were first developed following Columbine, SWAT officers were tapped to develop the curriculum because they were the experts in this type of tactical situation (Blair et al., 2013). Because the dump was the preferred style of entry for most tactical teams, the dump style of entry was incorporated into many active shooter programs.

However, patrol officers are not SWAT officers; one of the major differences is that patrol officers receive much less training and practice in tactical skills. The training and practice that patrol officers acquire in an active shooter class may be the only tactical training that the officers receive (outside of the academy) in their entire careers. Additionally, tactical teams train together so that they get to know and trust each other. It is not uncommon during active shooter events for police officers from multiple agencies to respond. These officers frequently have not trained together and may never have met before they arrived at the scene of the attack (Blair et al., 2013).

Some trainers, based upon their training experiences, began to argue that SWAT tactics were not appropriate for patrol officers responding to active shooter situations (Blair et al., 2013). Among their observations was the fact that that ad hoc teams of patrol officers often were unable to correctly execute the dump. Common problems included the first officer stopping in the doorway to engage a threat so that the rest of the team could not get into the room; the first officer entering the room and not being followed by the rest of the team; and officers not covering their areas of primary responsibility (p. 134–137). These trainers began to look for a style of entry that would be more effective for ad hoc teams of patrol officers. The style they selected was a variation of the slice.

2.2 THE SLICE

Slicing the pie has been widely taught as an effective method to conduct a deliberate search when there may be a suspect in a building but there is nothing driving the officers to move quickly (e.g., gunfire). Although there are some variations on exactly how the slicing is done, one common variation involves the first officer conducting the slice technique while the second officer stays in contact with the first officer to cover the areas of the hallway that have not yet been cleared (See Figure 2.2). If there are more than two officers, the other officers maintain cover in the sections of hallway that have already been cleared. Slicing simply means that the first officer slowly works his way from one side of the door to the other. As the officer moves, he can see bigger and bigger sections of the room (the pie slice shape of

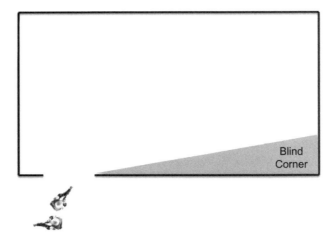

Figure 2.2 Slice method performed by two officers.

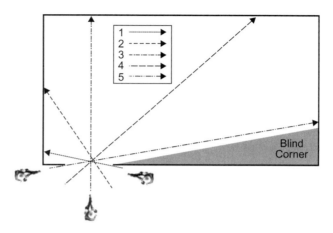

Figure 2.3 Slicing the pie, line of sight diagram.

these sections is where the slicing the pie terminology comes from). This is illustrated in Figure 2.3.

This process allows the officer to see a large majority of the room without having to enter the room. It should be noted that there will always be one corner of the room that the officer cannot see from the hallway when the door to the room is located near the corner of the room (this situation is referred to as a corner-fed room). There are two corners that cannot be seen if the door is located near the middle of one of the walls (this type of room is referred to as a center-fed room). Any corner that cannot be seen from outside of the room while slicing is referred to as a blind corner.

If the slice is done correctly, the slicing officer can often see a suspect before the suspect sees the officer. In this case, the slicing officer will often utilize hand signals to alert the other officers to the presence of the suspect and then two of the officers will slide out to deal with the suspect (See Figure 2.4).

If no suspect is seen from outside the room, the officers will need to enter the room to clear the blind corner. At this point, the entry is much like a dump. There are, however, two clear differences. First, the officers will have seen the general layout of the room and can plan their entry accordingly. Second, because the rest of the room has already been cleared, the officers can focus their attention on the blind corner when they make their entry.

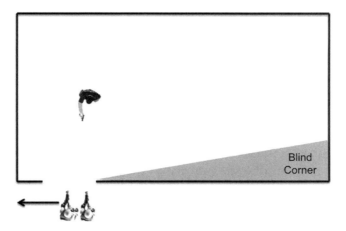

Figure 2.4 Slice method team threat engagement.

The slice, then, allows the officer to see the room in small sections and deal with the issues that are encountered in those sections while not exposing the officer to threats located in the sections of the room that cannot be seen. The officer also has the ability to control the pace of the slice and can slow down or speed up if needed. If a threat is detected, the officers can deal with the threat without having to enter the room and potentially expose themselves to other threats. Additionally, if the officers lose control of the situation, they can move away from the door to break contact with the threat.

While the traditional slice is conducted slowly, the variation taught for use during active shooter events, when shots are being fired, is not. We refer to this style of entry as a hasty slice. Because shots are being fired, two officers perform the slice, while standing shoulder to shoulder, to ensure that two guns are brought to bear on any suspect. The slice is also conducted quickly. While this does not provide the officers with the same level of safety that they have when they are conducting the traditional slice, it still allows the officers to confront the suspect without having to enter the room and expose themselves to other threats. Additionally, the officers can still break contact by stepping away from the door if they lose control of the situation. After any visible threats are dealt with from outside the doorway, the team can pause, assess the situation, and make a plan for dealing with the blind corner.

2.3 THE DEBATE

Proponents of the hasty slice argue that it overcomes some of the issues they have encountered when trying to train patrol officers to utilize the dump. First, they argue that when patrol officers execute a dump while facing hostile and armed suspects, all members of the team tend to focus on the suspect and not their areas of priority. This is a problem because if there is another threat in one of these ignored areas, the team will be exposed to the threat for some time before the team is aware that the threat is present. Second, proponents of the hasty slice argue that patrol officers executing the dump often stall in the doorway, preventing the other officers from entering the room to cover their assigned areas or supporting the other officer in the gunfight.

2.4 RELEVANT RESEARCH

Research into perception, threats, and actual police shootings has indicated that there are two sets of processes that typically occur when an officer is confronted with a threatening stimulus (e.g., a person with a gun). These are (1) the officer will experience an orienting response, and (2) the officer will experience an acute stress response. The effects of these responses are discussed below.

2.4.1 Orienting Response

Orienting responses (ORs) are important to the process of information processing. Sokolov, Sprinks, Näätäen, and Lyytinen (2002) present ORs as the building blocks of all investigatory processes. Orienting responses are reactions to a stimulus through which an individual becomes more sensitive to the stimulus. In humans, the reaction is generally one of inquisition. This is also true for animals. For instance, dogs exhibit a strong orienting response to new sounds by perking up their ears, turning their heads toward the sounds, and tensing their muscles.

Orienting responses have physiological effects. During an orienting response, the body readies itself to gather the most information possible about the potential threat/stimulus. A well-known physiological example of an orienting response is dilation of the pupil when light levels are reduced. The stimulus is the reduction of light and the orienting response is the dilation of the eye.

In terms of threats, the OR can have an inhibitory effect and halt the current behavior of the individual while acquiring data about the threat (e.g., armed suspect in a room; Sokolov et al., 2002). In other words, under certain conditions, an individual's OR will halt a conditioned response in order to gather additional information. Utilizing the example of an armed suspect in a room, upon entry, the officer's orienting response will activate to the observed threat and the conditioned movement may be halted to allow the brain to gather information. In most cases, the presence of a novel stimulus or threat will automatically trigger an orienting response (Sokolov et al., 2002). In the case of a room entry, this means that officers will automatically look at (orient on) a threat detected during the entry.

Because the orienting response that we are most concerned with involves vision, a more detailed discussion of the visual system in humans is warranted. The visual system is a complicated mechanism composed of six extraocular muscles and the millions of light-sensitive sensors, called rod and cone receptors, which make up the retina of the eye. Cone receptors are responsible for high-acuity color vision. Rod receptors lack detail and color capabilities but do respond to motion and light (Williams, Davids, & Williams, 2000). The retina utilizes the cone and rod receptors to transform light into nerve signals. The nerve signals travel to the visual cortex located in the occipital lobe at the back of the brain. It is here where the images are processed (Ungerleider & Mishkin, 1982).

The quality of vision is dependent on where the imagery is concentrated on the retina. For optimal acuity, the lens system directs light onto a small position with the densest concentration of cone and rod receptors. This location is called the fovea centralis (fovea). Light that contacts the fovea accounts for the clearest vision (Williams et al., 2000). Furthermore, acuity drops rapidly as imagery moves away from the optimal angular distance of the fovea—1 to 2 degrees of arc (i.e., the width of the thumb with the arm fully extended covers approximately 2 degrees of arc). Ruch (1965) found that acuity falls to 50% at 2.5 degrees, 25% at 7.5 degrees, and 4% in the furthest periphery.

As an object is detected in the periphery, the eye reorients itself to provide more detailed information about the object. This means that the position of the eye changes to place the image of the object of interest on the fovea. Researchers have empirically found the amount of time spent fixating on an object is correlated to the amount of information gathered and/or the complexity of the image (Just & Carpenter, 1976; Williams et al., 2000).

If a potential threat is detected in the periphery of the officer's vision during a room entry, the orienting response will automatically reorient the eye to place the image of the potential threat on the fovea in order to gather better information about the possible threat. In short, the natural tendency of the entering officer will be to look at the threat. In some cases, the orienting response may be strong enough that it halts other behaviors (e.g., moving) in order to maximize the information acquired. If this occurs, the officer may momentarily stop (stall) in his current position to gather more information.

The orienting response to a stimulus can be overcome through a process called habituation (Sokolov et al., 2002). Early habituation experiments were concerned with habituating animals to sounds. The animals were placed in a soundproof enclosure and an audible stimulus was engaged. At first, the animals would have an orienting response to the sounds. However, after repeated exposure to the stimulus, the orienting response disappeared.

This same process can occur in police training. Officers can be repeatedly exposed to a stimulus in order to habituate them to the stimulus and overcome the orienting response. In a dump room entry, for example, the officers can be repeatedly exposed to a threat upon entry and told to maintain their focus on their areas of responsibility. Over enough trials, this may allow the officer to overcome their natural tendency to orient on (look at) the threat.

2.4.2 Acute Stress Response

While the orienting response will naturally tend to draw an officer's attention to threats, there is another process that is also important. This process is acute stress response. Acute stress response is a set of physiological changes that occur as a result of a perceived threat. This process is also sometimes referred to as the fight, flight, or freeze response. Some of these physiological changes include increasing the heart rate to improve blood flow, tensing muscles to prepare for quick movement, and dilating the eyes to increase imagery light. The response is dependent on perception and training; specifically, how serious the officer perceives the threat to be and how quickly the officer's training is recalled determines how he or she responds to a threat. The level of stress also affects how well the officer is able to perform.

Grossman and Christensen (2008) spend considerable time discussing the harmful effects of stress on an officer. The authors discuss stress and performance along a color-coded, sliding scale. White and yellow are attributed to a state of rest and partial arousal. These are generally seen with a heart rate below 115 BPM. A level red reflects optimal performance with a BPM up to 145. At this level, the heart's output perfectly fuels the brain, muscles, and necessary organs for optimal performance. After this level, things begin to deteriorate. These levels are known as gray and black. At this level of physical stress, fine motor skills diminish. The body also undergoes a widespread vasoconstriction. Blood stops flowing to the hands and eventually the major muscle groups are deprived of precious oxygen. These physiological processes attributed to acute stress response also produce a number of psychological and physiological distortions.

Substantial research into the rare occasions when police utilize deadly force has revealed that the acute stress response often produces distortions in the perceptions of officers involved in shootings. The three most researched distortions are tunnel vision, audio exclusion, and time distortion. Tunnel vision occurs when the peripheral vision is no longer perceived. Officers experiencing tunnel vision only register visual input for images that are in the fovea. Audio exclusion (i.e., auditory blunting) results in an officer lacking the ability to hear what is happening during the situation. Time distortions involve the officer perceiving the event as occurring either faster or slower than normal (Solomon & Horn, 1986; Campbell, 1992, Klinger & Brunson, 2009).

In his study of 167 officers involved in shootings, Campbell (1992) found that 44% experienced tunnel vision, 42% experienced auditory blunting, and 34% experienced slow-motion time. A study conducted by Artwohl and Christensen (1997) was largely consistent with Campbell's study, but Artwohl and Christensen also identified new forms of perceptual distortion, including intensified sound and heightened visual detail. These occurred in 16% and 72% of the cases, respectively.

The most recent research into perceptual distortion was completed by Klinger and Brunson (2009). The authors established a snowball sample of 80 officers (113 total incidents) who had shot citizens in the line of duty. They found varying levels of auditory blunting in 82% of cases. Fifty-one percent reported tunnel vision, while 56% reported heightened visual acuity. Slow-motion time was experienced by 56% of the officers and fast-motion time occurred in 23% of the cases. The authors also studied the temporal variability of perceptual distortion to determine if the distortion occurred prior to shooting or during the shooting. Tunnel vision occurred prior to firing in 31% of cases and during firing in 27% of cases. Auditory blunting occurred prior to firing in 42% of cases and during firing in 70%. In all, 87% of officers reported some form of perceptual distortion before shooting and 92% during a shooting (Klinger & Brunson, 2009).

2.4.3 Application to the Entry Styles

The orienting response suggests that officers might pause when conducting either a dump or slice style entry. If the stall happens during the initial slice movement (while the officers are still on the other side of the threshold), the position of the first officer will generally be far enough away from the side of the door to allow a second officer to fire, so the momentary stall still allows another officer to support/cover the first officer and does not pose much of a problem. If the stall happens during the entry part of the dump, it does create a problem, as the other officers will be kept from entering the room and supporting the first officer or covering their areas of responsibility. Of course, a stall could also happen during the part of the slice when the officers enter the room to address the blind corner. We believe that it will be less likely to occur during the entry part of the slice because the officers will have had time to prepare for their entry and are more ready to deal with a threat than officers performing the dump.

Differences between the entries could also occur in regard to how threats are handled. We expect that officers conducting either a dump or a slice style of entry will experience both the orienting response and acute stress response when they are confronted with a suspect who is firing at them. When there is a single threat, we would expect officers to perform similarly when using either style, as they can be expected to focus on and handle the threat. The situation is different, however, if there is more than one threat. The difference is that while we expect officers conducting the slice style of entry to orient on the first suspect and experience acute stress response, as well as the accompanying perceptual distortions, these will occur while the officers are not exposed to the second threat (because the officers are still outside of the room). The officers will be able to deal with the first threat and then pause to recover from the orienting and acute stress responses. During this pause, the officers can form a plan about how to deal with the area(s) that they have not seen from outside the doorway. This allows the officers to immediately respond to a second threat located in the blind corner when the team enters the room.

When officers perform a dump, we expect them to orient on the first threat that they see. This will cause the second, third, and fourth officers to ignore their areas of responsibility and focus on the first threat. If there is a second threat in the blind corner, the officers executing a dump will take longer to identify and respond to this threat than officers who utilize the slice. We tested this hypothesis using the experiment discussed in the next chapter.

CHAPTER 3

Dump v. Slice Experiment

This experiment was designed to compare the performance of officers executing a dump style entry to those executing a slice entry. Because part of the debate about the effectiveness of these entries revolves around the ability of officers to cover their respective areas when they are exposed to a threat, it was necessary to utilize a design that would capture differences in the ability to cover areas of responsibility.

In this experiment, two "suspects" were placed in the room that officers entered. The first stood in the middle of the room and was actively shooting. The officers could see this suspect from the doorway. The second suspect was placed in the blind corner of the room. This suspect could not be seen until the officers entered the room, and the second suspect did not start shooting until the officers entered the room.

Based upon our review of the literature, we believed that the suspect standing in the middle of the room and firing would be perceived as a threat to the officers and that this threat would trigger a number of typically observed stress responses. More specifically, we believed that the officers would orient themselves to the threat (Sokolov et al., 2002) and experience tunnel vision (Solomon & Horn, 1986; Campbell, 1992; Klinger & Brunson, 2009). We expected this to occur in both types of entry; however, as discussed previously, orienting and tunneling do not pose as much of a problem for officers performing the slice. The slicing officers can deal with the first suspect from outside of the room, pause to recover from the stress response, make a plan to enter the room, and then enter and deal with the second suspect.

We believed the situation for officers executing a dump would be substantially different. As the officers executed the dump, they were faced with a gunman who was shooting at them. We believed that this would cause all officers entering the room to look at and turn to face (orient on) this threat. The stress of the situation would also cause tunnel vision, which would reduce the officers' ability to detect other threats. We suspected that officers would focus on the first threat and ignore their areas of responsibility. As a result, it would take officers in the dump conditions longer to detect the second suspect. This would mean that officers in the dump conditions would be exposed to fire from the second suspect for longer than officers in the slice conditions.

We also examined whether or not the first officer to enter the room stopped in the doorway (i.e., stalled before entering the room), thus delaying the other officers from entering. Because of the orienting and stress responses discussed above, we believed that officers in the dump conditions would be more likely to stop their forward motion and stall in the doorway. A more detailed discussion of the experiment is presented in this chapter.

3.1 METHOD

Participants were recruited from nine active shooter training classes conducted by Advanced Law Enforcement Rapid Response Training (ALERRT). ALERRT, affiliated with the Texas State University School of Criminal Justice, has conducted active shooter training classes since 2002, and to date, has trained more than 50,000 officers from across the country. One hundred and ninety-nine participants completed the study. Most of the participants (85%) were certified peace officers in the state of Texas. Those who were not certified peace officers included federal law enforcement agents, military personnel, and a few tactical medics. Participants ranged from 23 to 59 years old (Mean (M) = 36.1, Standard Deviation (SD) = 7.9). Years of policing experience ranged from 0 to 38 (M = 9.0, SD = 8.4). Most of the participants (72%) did not have any tactical (SWAT) experience.

Participants self-selected into teams consisting of three or four officers during the training class. These groups were then randomly assigned to perform either the dump or slice entry. Random assignment is important because it evens out differences in ability levels, skills, and other factors that could hide the effects of the entries on the outcome measures. Randomly assigning participants to groups also allows us to use a variety of statistical tests to assess whether the observed differences are likely the product of chance errors or the existence of a real effect. These tests also allow us to assess the size of the differences.

After assignment, a certified ALERRT instructor explained and demonstrated the assigned entry to the group (the groups had previously been exposed to both types of entry during the training class). Each group was then given the chance to practice the entry five times. The instructor gave feedback to the group after each practice run. All suspects and innocents in the scenario were played either by ALERRT staff or Texas State University students.

Following the practice sessions, the participants were issued force-on-force pistols and safety masks. The force-on-force pistols are real pistols that have been re-chambered to fire a special marking cartridge. Next, the participants were introduced to the scenario for the experiment. They were told that they had received a call of shots fired at school, and they were the first responding officers on the scene. The experimenter pointed in the direction that the team would be moving and told the group that the experiment would start when they heard shots being fired.

When the experimenter called the scenario "hot," the first "suspect" began firing his blank pistol to start the run. The study participants then moved down a short hallway and encountered the study room. Two study rooms were utilized during the course of the experiment. These rooms were very similar with the exception that one room opened to the right and the other to the left. This means that the door was in the right hand corner of one room and the left hand corner of the other. During each run, there were three role-players in the room. The first was Suspect 1, who stood in the middle of the room directly in front of the door and fired a blank gun. The second was Suspect 2, who stood in the blind corner of the room, was armed with a force-on-force pistol, and began firing at the officers about one second after the officers made entry into the room. The final was an innocent person. This innocent person was included to force the officers to make correct shoot/don't shoot determinations while under stress. The layout of the room and positioning of the suspects is presented in Figure 3.1.

The scenario ended when the team made entry into the room and shot both suspects. At this time, the experimenter called "cease fire," conducted a short debriefing, and thanked the participants for their time. If the entry team shot at the innocent person in the room, the experimenter recorded that at this time as well.

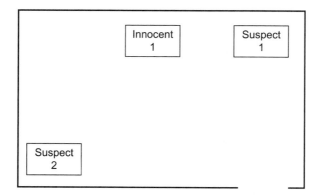

Figure 3.1 Room layout.

3.2 CODING

The participant groups executed a total of 52 entries. Twenty-seven of these were slices and 25 were dumps. Three of the dump entries and two of the slice entries were excluded from analysis because the participants failed to follow instructions (i.e., the group executed an entry type other than the one to which they had been assigned). To ensure that the coders' judgments were reliable, one coder assessed all of the entries and a second coder evaluated 25% of the entries.

Three variables were coded. The first was exposure time. This was the amount of time that passed from when any part of the first officer to enter the experiment room crossed the threshold of the doorway until the second suspect was detected and fired upon. The coders were in perfect agreement on this variable for 75% of the cases. In the three cases when there was some disagreement, the differences ranged from 1/30th of a second to one half of a second.

The second variable was stalling in the doorway. If the first officer paused or stopped while entering the room and there was no room for another officer to enter, this was coded as a stall. The agreement of the coders on this variable was 100%.

The third coded variable was arc of fire violations. In firearms training, officers are taught several basic firearms safety rules that apply in all firearms situations. One of these is that the officers must be aware of what is in their arc of fire. This applies to both the area between the officer and the intended target and to what is behind the intended target. If there is something in the officer's arc of fire that the officer does not want to shoot, the officer must either hold fire or change position so that the arc is clear. We noticed that during the scenario, officers would often violate this safety rule and shoot when another officer was in their arc of fire, so a post hoc decision was made to code these events. These events were coded as a dichotomous violation/no violation variable. The coders agreed on this judgment 92% of the time.

3.3 RESULTS

3.3.1 Exposure Time
Our belief was that officers who were executing the dump entry in this experiment would take longer to detect and deal with the second gunman than officers who were executing the slice. The exposure time (the time before the second suspect was shot at) for officers in the slice conditions was 1.2 seconds (see Figure 3.2). In the dump scenario, it was 2.7 seconds. Statistical tests suggested that this difference was unlikely to be the result of chance and that the magnitude of the difference was large (the relevant tests are presented in notes under the relevant figures throughout this section).

3.3.2 Stalling in the Door
Stalling in the doorway occurred in 0 of the 23 (0%) slice entries and 4 of the 22 (18%) dump entries (see Figure 3.3). This difference was large enough that it was unlikely to be the result of chance error and suggested the difference between the entries was moderate.

3.3.3 Arc of Fire Violations
Arc of fire violations occurred in 3 of the 25 (12%) slice entries and 13 of 22 (59%, see Figure 3.4) dump entries. This difference was large enough that it was unlikely to be the product of chance and suggested that the effect of entry type on arc of fire violations was large.

3.3.4 Innocents Shot
The innocent person in the room was shot at in 25% of the runs. This occurred in eight of the 25 slice runs and four of the 22 dump runs (see Figure 3.5). While this difference may appear large in the chart, it is not large enough to rule out that it occurred by chance. In fact, we would expect to see a difference this large or larger about one third of the time if the type of entry did not affect the likelihood of the

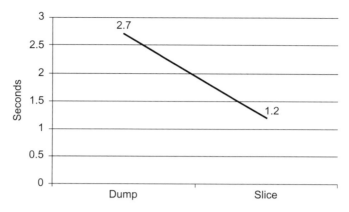

Figure 3.2 Exposure time. Note: $F_{(1,45)} = 29.29$, $p < .001$, $\eta^2 = .39$.

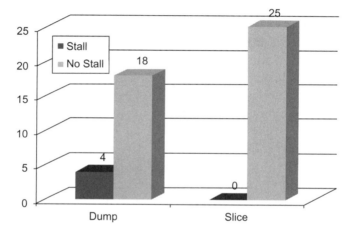

*Figure 3.3 **Stalls in the doorway.** Note: Fisher's exact test $p = .04$, $\varphi = .33$.*

innocent person being shot. The statistical tests also showed that the magnitude of this difference was small.

3.3.5 Between Room Differences

Because of scheduling conflicts, the experiment was conducted in two separate rooms. The first three days were conducted in the first room and the other six were conducted in the second room. As was mentioned previously, the rooms were similar in design, except for that the first room opened to the officers' right and the second to their left.

To examine whether the room impacted exposure times, we conducted a more sophisticated test called a two-way ANOVA. The results of this

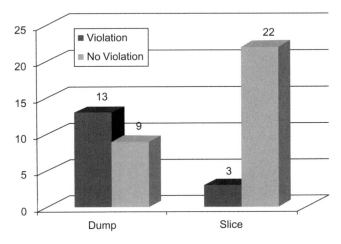

*Figure 3.4 **Arc of fire violations.** Note: $X^2_{(1)} = 11.56$, p < .001, $\varphi = .50$.*

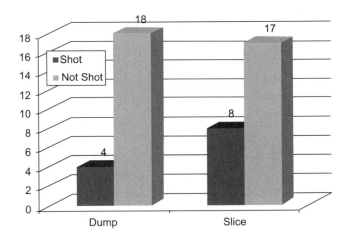

*Figure 3.5 **Innocent person shot.** Note: $X^2_{(1)} = 1.18$, p = .33, $\varphi = .16$.*

test suggested that while the dump produced longer average exposures than the slice, the combination of the second room and the dump seemed to produce exceptionally long exposure times (see Figure 3.6).

3.4 DISCUSSION

The results of this experiment clearly supported our hypothesis that the dump type entry would produce longer exposure times than the slice. It took participants in the dump conditions an average of 1.5 seconds

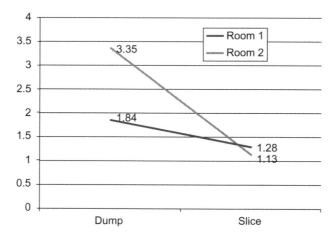

Figure 3.6 **Mean exposure time by entry and room.** *Note: Main effect for entry type – $F_{(1,43)} = 28.58$, $p < .001$ $\eta^2 = .29$; Main effect for room – $F_{(1,43)} = 6.77$, $p < .05$, $\eta^2 = .07$; Interaction between room and entry – $F_{(1,43)} = 9.99$, $p < .01$, $\eta^2 = .10$.*

longer to detect and engage the second suspect than participants in the slice conditions. While 1.5 seconds may seem like a short time to people who are unfamiliar with gunfights, it is an extremely long time when someone is firing at you. The participants in the dump conditions frequently did not detect and engage the second suspect until the suspect had fired all 15 rounds from his magazine and was in the process of reloading. This never happened in the slice conditions. Another way to look at this data is in relative terms. It took participants in the dump conditions more than twice as long to respond to the second shooter as it took participants in the slice conditions.

We also found that the first officer stalled in 18% of the dump style entries and never stalled during the slice style entries. We believe this is a function of the orienting response discussed in the previous chapter. When performing a slice entry, officers are able to observe approximately 85% of the room prior to physically entering the room. The officers can also plan their entry and prepare to confront someone in the corner. However, we believe the first officer on a dump entry may become overwhelmed by the sheer amount of information he or she is required to process.

The slice also appeared to produce better outcomes in regard to arc of fire violations. Arc of fire violations occurred in 12% of the slice entries and 59% of the dump entries. Arc of fire violations, then, were almost 5 times more common in dump entries than slice entries. While we did not observe any incidents in which one of the officers shot another officer (this was detectable because the officers utilized a different color force-on-force round than the suspects), the results of such an occurrence in the field would be profound. Such blue-on-blue incidents are a major concern in the police community (New York State Task Force on Police-On-Police Shootings, 2010; Force Science #215, #216), and the basic firearms safety rules exist to prevent them.

In our estimation, the same processes produce both the increased exposure time and arc of fire violations in the dump condition. The force-on-force scenario is somewhat threatening to the participant officers. When they encounter the first suspect firing at them through the door, the officers naturally orient on that threat. They also likely experience a variety of stress-related phenomena such as tunnel vision and audio exclusion. This happens regardless of the entry style that is used. The differences in exposure time and arc of fire happen because of the different structures of the entries.

During the dump entry, the officers encounter a suspect firing at them as they enter the room. They naturally orient on this threat to deal with it. They also likely experience tunnel vision and audio exclusion. The result of this is that the second, third, and fourth officers, who should be clearing the areas of the room that were not addressed by the first officer, drop their areas of responsibility and focus completely on the suspect who is firing at them. This focus lasts until the officers hear or start to feel the impact of the rounds being fired by the second suspect (in our observations of the videos, it appears to be the impact of the rounds that the officers notice first). When this occurs, the officers turn and immediately engage the threat. Because they are under stress and experiencing tunnel vision, the officers do not see that there is another officer in their arc of fire unless that officer physically obstructs the firing officer's ability to see the target.

In the slice, the officers orient on and engage the first suspect from the other side of the threshold. This means that while the officers are focused on the first threat and experiencing tunnel vision, they are not exposed to the second threat. After the officers deal with the first threat, they can pause, assess the situation, and plan how to deal with the blind corner. The more skilled teams then performed an entry in which the first officer to enter the room was looking at the blind corner immediately when he or she entered the room and was therefore able to immediately assess and deal with the second suspect. The first officer in the less skilled teams would sometimes look at the area of the room that had already been cleared when entering, but the second officer to enter would then enter looking at the blind corner that contained the second suspect. This produced lower exposure times. There were also fewer arc of fire violations because the team of officers did not suddenly turn to engage a new threat while under stress.

We also found that the dump exposure time was longer in the second room than in the first. Because this was not a design feature of the experiment, we can't be certain what produced this difference. It may have been a product of differences in skill levels of the officers in the runs or the particular layout of the rooms, for example. Nevertheless, the finding that during the dump average exposure varied by room but did not during the slice is interesting. It suggests that the slice may be a more consistent style of entry than the dump. Of course, additional research is needed to verify this as well as to try to identify what specifically caused the differences.

The only measure where the slice does not appear to have been superior to the dump is in regard to innocents being shot. In our sample, we observed about twice as many cases of officers shooting at innocents in the slices as compared to the dumps (8 and 4, respectively). A few comments on this are warranted. First, there were a few more slice entries than dumps, so we would expect to see slightly more innocents shot at in the slices than the dumps. Second, the difference that we observed was not large enough for us to feel confident that it was not the product of chance. While random assignment does even out the differences between groups, it does not do so perfectly; so, we expect to see some variation in the performances of the groups based upon this assignment error. To correct for this, we require the difference between the groups to be of a certain size before we feel confident enough to say that we think there is a "real" difference between the groups. In the case of the number of innocents shot, this difference was not large enough for us to feel confident in saying that we think it is a "real" difference. In fact, we expect to see a difference this large or larger about one third of the time that we conduct this number of observations and there is no "real" effect. Additionally, there are no reports of officers responding to active shooter events and shooting innocent people despite the fact that many of these responding officers have been trained to use the slice. Finally, we did not see anything in the research literature to suggest that there would be a difference in the number of innocents shot depending on the entry. When considering all of this information, we do not feel confident in saying that the slice produces more innocents shot than the dump. But we do think that it is an issue that is worthy of additional exploration.

Taken as a whole, the results of this experiment support the use of the slice. It resulted in less exposure time, fewer arc of fire violations, and a smaller number of stalls, while not significantly affecting the number of incorrect shoot/don't shoot decisions. It may also be a more consistent entry.

This being said, a few caveats are in order. First, this experiment was specifically designed to examine the impact of multiple threats on the performance of officers during the entries. In cases where there is a single threat (which is common in active shooter events), entry type should not affect the performance measures assessed here, with the exception of the stall.

Second, most of the officers in this study did not have experience as tactical officers, and the teams they formed had very limited practice time together. It is possible that, with practice and experience, the effects of a threat on the performance of the dumps observed here can be overcome. This is the essence of the habituation findings in the orienting response literature (Sokolov et al., 2002). A SWAT team that regularly practices may be able to overcome the natural tendency to orient on a threat and cover their respective areas, producing exposure times that are consistent with those produced by the slice (many SWAT officers that we have spoken to insist that this is the case); however, we would like to point out that this means conducting training specifically to overcome a natural instinct, and this process is likely to take considerable effort and time. In the case of patrol officers, who are likely to be the first on the scene during an active

shooter event, the officers are unlikely to receive the amount of training that is needed to overcome these natural instincts.

With these caveats in mind, we think it is clear that the slice is a
better style of entry to teach to patrol officers during active shooter
training. The structure of the slice does not attempt to overcome
the officer's natural tendencies. It allows these tactically less-
experienced officers to deal with the problem in smaller pieces and provides the officers with more time to think through the situation.
For these reasons, the specific entries tested in the other studies
presented in this book are conducted using a slice style.

Accepting the cognitive limitations of people and modifying the
way that something is done is similar to how researchers in the ecological rationality paradigm deal with decision-making errors (Gigerenzer,
2008; Rieskamp & Reimer, 2007). This approach sees human behavior
as being similar to a pair of scissors (Simon, 1956). One blade of the
scissors represents the cognitive capabilities or processes of the actor
and the other the structure of the environment. Just as it is not possible
to understand how a pair of scissors operates by studying a single
blade, it is also not possible to understand how human decisions
are made without studying the structure of the environment in addition
to the capabilities of the actor.

When researchers in the ecological rationality paradigm discover
that people's judgments are not accurate in a particular environment,
they will usually attempt to alter the structure of the environment
rather than the cognitive capabilities or processes of the actor. This is
because the environment is usually much more malleable than a
cognitive process that has developed over years, decades, or millennia
(Gigerenzer, 2008).

In the case of the entry styles examined here, there are clear cognitive processes in operation. Officers will naturally orient on threats.
They will also tend to experience acute stress response (ASR).
ASR frequently produces a variety of perceptual distortions including
tunnel vision and audio exclusion. The styles of entry can be considered to be the environmental structures. While it may be possible to
conduct enough training to overcome the cognitive limitations of the

officers (this is the point of much tactical training; Friedland & Keinan, 1992), it is easier to alter the entry style (i.e., structure of the environment) to one that is better adapted to the situation. This approach has also been suggested in other policing situations, such as how investigators can better detect deception (Blair, Levine, Reimer, & McCluskey, 2012). We now turn to discussing the specific entry techniques that dictate exactly where the officers go when they enter the room.

CHAPTER 4

Room Entry Techniques Overview

In the last chapter, we presented data that suggested that the slice style of entry was more effective than the dump style of entry. In this chapter, we explore variations of the slice entry and literature related to its effectiveness. It should be noted that, though we will be discussing these entry types from the slice point of view, the major difference between these entries is the direction that the first officer to enter the room moves. Because of this, these entries can also be executed from the dump style setup. Additionally, all of the entries are presented as being done with two-person teams. This was done because the actions of the first two entering officers are critical to the arguments advanced by the proponents of the various techniques. The entries can be executed with larger teams. If they are, the additional team members fill the spaces that are left open by the first two officers. We begin by discussing the different entry variations. Next, we identify the major points of debate regarding the merits and weaknesses of the entries. Finally, we review research literature that is relevant to the arguments and develop predictions about how officers will perform when using the techniques. Chapter 5 presents a series of experiments to test these predictions.

4.1 UNKNOWN ENTRY

The unknown entry is referred to as the unknown because the first officer to enter the room moves directly toward the part of the room that was not seen (i.e., the blind corner) while slicing the pie (see Figure 4.1; see Chapter 2 for a discussion of slicing the pie). The second officer proceeds laterally into the room behind the first officer. It should be noted that while the second officer is moving into the room, he or she is not looking straight ahead; rather, the second officer looks first to the blind corner because that is the area of the room that has not been seen from the hallway.

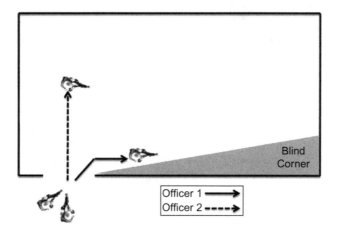

Figure 4.1 Unknown entry.

4.2 KNOWN ENTRY

In the known entry, the first officer to enter moves directly toward the area that he or she has already seen and, thus, knows is cleared (see Figure 4.2). It should again be noted that the officer is looking first at the blind corner. The officer is, therefore, looking in one direction but moving in another. The second officer moves directly toward the blind corner upon entry. The known entry is simply the unknown entry executed in reverse order.

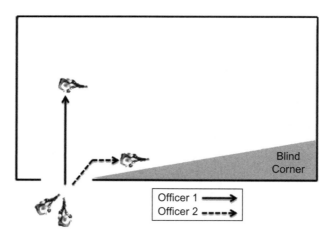

Figure 4.2 Known entry.

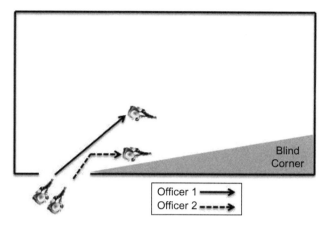

Figure 4.3 Hybrid entry.

4.3 HYBRID ENTRY

We refer to the third entry technique as the hybrid entry because it blends elements of the other two techniques. In this technique, the first officer to enter moves at about a 45-degree angle to the blind corner (see Figure 4.3). The second officer moves directly toward the blind corner.

4.4 THE DEBATE

The advantages/disadvantages of these techniques have been the subject of intense debate among police officers. Unfortunately, these debates have not been informed by empirical evidence. Instead, they have taken place informally among the supporters and detractors of the techniques. The most common arguments were discussed by Blair et al. (2013) and are summarized below.

Supporters of the unknown entry technique argue that this technique gives the first officer into the room the best shooting accuracy. This is because the officer is moving directly toward the threat and the threat is becoming a larger target as the officer advances. The belief is that accuracy is more important than other issues because the officer can best protect him or herself by shooting and disabling a hostile suspect as quickly as possible (Blair et al., 2013).

Supporters of the known entry technique argue that the unknown entry technique has several disadvantages. The first is that, because the suspect is waiting in the room, he or she will be able to fire before the entering officer. This is because the officer has to enter, scan for threats, assess the threat, decide to shoot or not, and then shoot, while the suspect simply sees someone come through the door and shoots (Blair et al., 2013).

The supporters of the known entry technique argue that this means the first officer must assume that he or she will not fire first and instead should be concerned with making the shots of the suspect less accurate. The lateral movement, relative to the suspect in the corner, is assumed to reduce the accuracy of the suspect's shots. Relatedly, supporters of the known entry technique argue that the shot accuracy advantage created when the officer moves directly toward the suspect in the unknown entry also applies to the suspect. That is, the suspect gets more accurate as the first officer in the unknown entry advances toward the suspect. The first officer in the unknown entry is believed to be more likely to be hit, and be hit more often, than the first officer in the known entry (Blair et al., 2013).

Second, critics of the unknown entry technique argue that because the second officer to enter the room must move behind the first officer (through the suspect's field of fire), the second officer might be hit by shots intended for the first officer. That is, misses on the first officer (or bullets that over-penetrate and pass through the first officer) could become hits on the second officer (Blair et al., 2013).

Third, critics of the unknown entry technique argue that because the second officer must move behind and far enough past the first officer to fire safely, the second officer will be slower to fire at the suspect. This is important because the second officer must disable the suspect in the event that the first officer is incapacitated upon entry (Blair et al., 2013).

The primary critique of the known entry is that this entry reduces the accuracy of the first officer to enter the room. The argument is that while the lateral movement of the officer reduces the suspect's accuracy, it also reduces the officer's accuracy. This has led some critics of the known entry technique to refer to the technique as the "rabbit" because the purpose of the first officer is to draw the fire of a hostile suspect while the second officer disables the suspect (Blair et al., 2013).

Supporters of the hybrid entry technique argue that it possesses the strengths of both the unknown and known entry techniques. The slightly lateral movement of the first officer is believed to reduce suspect accuracy while not reducing officer accuracy. The entry of the second officer directly toward the blind corner is believed to be faster than the entry of the second officer behind the first in the unknown entry and also would not expose the second officer to fire aimed at the first officer (Blair et al., 2013).

The debate, then, can be summarized as consisting of four issues:

1. Can the first officer to enter be expected to fire before the suspect?
2. Do the entry techniques affect the accuracy of the suspect and first officer's fire?
3. Do the entry techniques affect the speed at which the second officer can fire?
4. Does the second officer get hit by fire intended for the first officer when executing the unknown entry?

4.5 RELEVANT LITERATURE

4.5.1 Can the First Officer to Enter Expect to Fire Before the Suspect?

There is much literature on reaction time that relates directly to this issue. Overall, these studies indicate that reaction time increases as the complexity of the situation increases (Luce, 1986). For example, a simple reaction (e.g., fire a weapon when a light flashes) is faster than a choice-based reaction (e.g., fire a weapon only at hostile targets mixed with non hostile targets). The actual physical movement time does not significantly vary; rather, the time it takes to choose an action slows the overall reaction time. Welford (1980) also found that reaction time is slowed if distractions are present. A multitude of studies have found reaction time improves with practice (Ando, Kida, & Oda, 2002, 2004; Rogers, Johnson, Martinez, Mille, & Hedman, 2003; Visser, Raijmakers, & Molenaar, 2007).

These general findings suggest how an officer would perform when making a room entry. A room entry is a complex event that is also full of distractions. This would suggest that an officer would be slower in these situations than a suspect who has fewer choices to consider and is not distracted by irrelevant information.

There are also several reaction time studies that have specifically examined police officer reaction times in shooting situations. Lewinski and Hudson (2003) found a mean reaction time of .31 seconds for officers to shoot once prompted by a flashing light. The actual response (i.e., pulling the trigger) took only .08 seconds, while the average time to process the prompt took .23 seconds, or three fourths of the total reaction time. Lewinski and Hudson went on to study reaction times when complexity was added. In this study, the complexity involved different sequences of lights. The officers were instructed to fire in response to some sequences and told to hold fire in response to others. In these more complex scenarios, the officers took an average of .56 seconds to react and made mental errors that were not present in the simple reaction scenario (i.e., 9% shot when they shouldn't have and 4% did not shoot when they should have; Lewinski & Hudson, 2003).

Blair et al. (2012) studied reaction speed in a force-on-force scenario. In this study, a law enforcement officer faced an armed suspect who had his weapon either by his side or pointed at his own head. The officer had his weapon aimed at the suspect and gave commands to put the gun down. In some conditions, the suspect would comply. In others, the suspect would attempt to shoot the officer. In the shooting conditions, the officer would attempt to shoot the suspect before the suspect shot the officer. Blair et al. (2012) found that highly trained officers (the sample consisted of SWAT team members at a training conference) fired their weapons at the same time or slower than the suspect in 61% of encounters. This was despite the fact that the officer was already aiming his or her gun at the suspect and the suspect had to bring his or her gun into firing position before shooting. The officer's process of perceiving the suspect's movement, deciding on a response, and performing the response was generally slower than the suspect's action of bringing the gun on target and firing. The findings of this study specifically suggest that police officers performing room entries will be slower to act than suspects.

This suggestion is reinforced by the literature on the decision-making process. In the tactical world, this process is often explained using Boyd's Cycle (Boyd, 1995). Boyd's Cycle consists of four distinct steps that all people in competition with each other go through when taking action.

- The first is observe. The person must see or sense what is happening.
- The second is orientation. The person must put what she or he has seen into context.
- The third is decision. The person must choose the action the he or she will take.
- The fourth is the action. The person must do what he or she has decided to do.

Together, the steps are referred to as the OODA loop. It is a loop because, after the action is taken, the process starts all over again. When people are opposing each other, this process is time competitive. The person who is able to maneuver through the loop the fastest will win.

This process is quite similar to the process described by Zeleny (1982). According to Zeleny (1982), the decision-making process consists of three phases (i.e., pre-decision, decision, and post-decision). Pre-decision involves gathering information and systematically evaluating potential actions and alternatives. Next, during the decision phase, the most beneficial actions are weighed against each other and the best viable decision is made. Throughout this phase, alternative actions are discarded until only one remains. The post-decision phase involves evaluating the decision performed and deciding if the action was correct. Following this evaluation, additional actions may be performed to accomplish the goal. Much like the OODA loop, after you gather information and make a decision, an evaluation of the decision begins. During the evaluation, the next three-part cycle begins.

When applied to room entries, the OODA loop suggests that the entering officer will be slower to act than a suspect who is already in the room. The entering officer must first scan the room to see if there are any potential threats. The officer must then put what he or she sees into context (e.g., There is a person with a gun. Are they behaving in a threatening manner? Are there other threats? Is it another police officer?). Then the officer must decide what action to take (e.g., shoot/don't shoot, give verbal commands, back out of the room, close distance). Finally, the officer must act.

The suspect who has already committed to shooting people has a much shorter process to navigate. The suspect must simply observe the officers entering the room and then shoot. The suspect has already done all of the orientation that is needed and decided on his or her course of action. Therefore, the OODA loop predicts that the suspect will be able to move through the cycle faster than the officer.

Given the reaction time and decision-making literature, we predict that officers will not generally be able to shoot before the suspects when conducting room entries. We test this hypothesis in the next chapter.

4.5.2 Do the Entry Techniques Affect Officer and Suspect Accuracy?

The second issue is indirectly addressed within the general literature on accuracy during police shootings. Several researchers have conducted post hoc analyses of police shootings to assess the accuracy of officers. For instance, White (2006) analyzed all 271 police-involved shooting events in Philadelphia between 1987 and 1992 and found that 51% of officers missed their target, 35% connected and injured their target, and only 14% of the shootings resulted in a fatality. Alpert and Dunham (1995) studied 190 firearm discharges within the Metro-Dade Police Department between 1988 and June 1994. They found that most officers' shots were taken within 30 feet, and only 32% of the intentional shots hit the intended target. Several other studies have reported a wide variety of accuracy rates—ranging from 23% to 56% (Horvath & Donahue, 1982; Pate & Hamilton, 1991; Fitzgerald & Bromley, 1998). The consistent finding is that officer accuracy during a shooting is generally low.

We were unable to locate any empirical literature that addressed the impact of specific movements on accuracy. There are, however, numerous pieces written by practitioners based on their personal experiences that are intended as training protocols. These pieces almost universally suggest that lateral movement on the part of the officer reduces both suspect and officer accuracy (Rayburn, 2004; Spaulding, 2010). Furthermore, Spaulding (2010) discusses the disadvantage of moving toward a target because the movement results in increased accuracy of the suspect. However, these claims have not been empirically tested. Nonetheless, we tentatively hypothesize that when officers move laterally, both their accuracy and the accuracy of the suspects will be reduced.

4.5.3 Do the Entry Techniques Affect the Speed with Which the Second Officer Can Fire?

There is not any literature that relates directly to the issue of how quickly someone can get into a firing position, but there are some standard firearms rules that can be applied to the issue. There are four generally recognized firearms safety rules (Morrison & Cooper, 1991). Two of the rules are directly related to this issue. The first is that the gun should never be pointed at anything that you are not willing to destroy, and the second is that you should be sure of your target and what is beyond it. When these rules are combined and applied to law enforcement, they create what is commonly referred to as the arc of fire. This arc of fire extends in an expanding cone from the end of the barrel of the officer's gun to the target and past it out to either the effective range of the weapon or the nearest solid barrier that is capable of stopping the bullet. If anyone is in the arc of fire that the officer does not want to shoot, the officer must not fire. Instead the officer must change position to ensure that the arc of fire contains only the desired target.

When applied to room entries, the arc of fire dictates how far the second officer must move before shooting. In both the known and hybrid entries, the second officer can begin firing as soon as he enters the room (see Figures 4.4 & 4.5). In the unknown entry, however, the second officer must move far enough past the first officer to ensure that the first officer is not in the arc of fire (see Figure 4.6). Because this distance is further than in the other two entries, it is logical to conclude that it will take longer for the second officer in unknown entries to fire upon the suspect. How much longer it takes is an empirical question that will be addressed in the research presented in the next chapter.

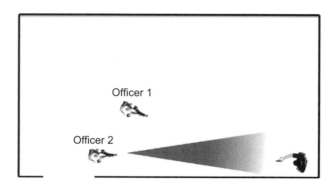

Figure 4.4 Arc of fire—hybrid entry.

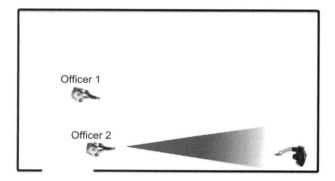

Figure 4.5 Arc of fire—known entry.

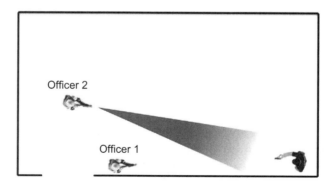

Figure 4.6 Arc of fire—unknown entry.

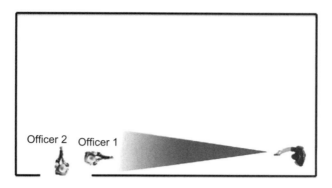

Figure 4.7 Suspect arc of fire during unknown entry.

4.5.4 Does the Second Officer Entering the Room During the Unknown Entry Get Hit by Rounds Intended for the First Officer?

The arc of fire also applies to the suspect's shots. It only stands to reason that if the suspect is shooting at the first officer and the second officer is in the suspect's arc of fire, the second officer may be hit. This situation occurs only when the second officer is passing behind the first during an unknown entry (see Figure 4.7). Given the low accuracies observed during actual gunfights, there are likely to be many rounds that go past the first officer and could potentially hit the second (Horvath & Donahue, 1982; Pate & Hamilton, 1991; Alpert & Dunham, 1995; Fitzgerald & Bromley, 1998; White, 2006). Additionally, in actual entries, bullets that hit the first officer and pass all the way through could also hit the second officer. Given this background, it is logical to conclude that the second officer may occasionally be hit when passing behind the first. The studies discussed in the next chapter will attempt to determine how often this happens.

CHAPTER 5

Room Entry Techniques Experiments

In this chapter, we examine the impact of three specific types of entries (known, unknown, and hybrid) on both officer and suspect performance. Because the debate surrounding the entries is complex, we conducted a number of studies to address specific issues. Experiment 1 was focused on the impact of the entry types on the accuracy of participants playing the role of hostile criminal suspects. This experiment also assessed the speed at which both the suspects and officers fired, and whether or not the second officer was hit while passing behind the first in the unknown entries. Experiment 2 examined the accuracy of the first officer entering the room. Experiment 3 sought to replicate the data on first officer accuracy in Experiment 2 and examine how quickly the second officer was able to fire. Experiment 4 sought to replicate the results from Experiments 1−3 and also assess the amount of time it took the first officer to fire during the entry.

5.1 EXPERIMENT 1

5.1.1 Methodology

Participants were recruited from criminal justice classes at a large southwestern university by offering course credit. Sixty-nine students participated. These students were mostly male (64%) and Caucasian (57%). The mean age of the students was 20.49 (SD = 2.32) years. None of the participants were licensed police officers.

The study was conducted at Advanced Law Enforcement Rapid Response Tactic's (ALERRT) training facility. Upon arrival, the participants participated in standard force-on-force safety preparations. This included searching the participants to ensure that no weapons were brought into the facility and a briefing on the safety rules for the use of force-on-force weapons. The weapons are actual firearms that have been re-chambered to fire a special marking round. The round is made of soap, leaves a mark when it hits, and is propelled by gunpowder. The rounds also sting when they strike unprotected areas. During this briefing, the participants were issued and instructed in the use of the safety equipment. Biographical information was also collected at this time. Participants were told that they were playing the role of a suspect who shot someone and fled into the study building. They are now hiding in the room and waiting to ambush the police officers that are searching for the suspect.

Following the briefing, participants were given the opportunity to fire five rounds at a target to familiarize themselves with the training pistol. A safety officer then placed a participant in the entry room. This room was rectangular in shape and had the door located in the northeast corner of the room. The suspect was always placed in the blind (southeast) corner of the room. The suspect was approximately 5 yards from the door. The safety officer verified that the study area was ready, inspected the participant's safety equipment to ensure it was properly attached, issued the force-on-force weapon, and declared the room hot. The same team of two highly experienced police officers then executed one of the three entries based upon a fully counterbalanced rotation. The officers controlled exactly when they conducted the entry. All of these exchanges were video recorded. Each suspect had four rounds to fire at the entering officers. Each officer on the entry team had three rounds.

After the engagement, the safety officer called cease-fire, collected the weapons, and inspected the officers for hits. He then escorted the officers out of the entry room into a safe room. The entry room was reset, and the officers executed the next assigned entry after the room was declared ready. This process was repeated until the officers had executed all three entries against a particular suspect.

To examine the reaction times of the suspects, the videos were loaded into a piece of video editing software that allowed the videos to be advanced one frame at a time. The frame rate on the videos was 30 per second. Two coders assessed the videos. The first coded all of the videos and the second coded 20% to provide a reliability check. The observed reliability for all of the measures was high.

Three variables were coded. The first was the time at which the first officer to enter the room crossed the threshold of the door. The second was the time at which the first officer fired his first shot, and the third was the time at which the suspect fired his or her first shot. Only 197 of the 207 runs were coded, because the cameras failed to capture the detail needed to produce all of the measures for some of the runs.

5.1.2 Results

Reaction time. To assess the reaction time of the suspects, we subtracted the time that the first officer crossed the threshold of the doorway from the time that the suspect fired his or her first shot. Suspects fired an average of .59 seconds (SD = .25) after the first officer crossed the threshold. To calculate the reaction time of the first officer, we subtracted the time that he crossed the threshold from the time that the first officer fired his first shot. The first officer fired an average of .55 seconds (SD = .13) after he crossed the threshold. We then subtracted the reaction time of the suspect from the reaction time of the officer to produce a difference score; thus, a positive number indicated that the suspect shot before the officer, and a negative number indicated that the officer shot first. The mean difference was − .037 seconds (SD = .27). These differences are presented in Figure 5.1. The average difference was too small to confidently conclude that it was not the product of random error.

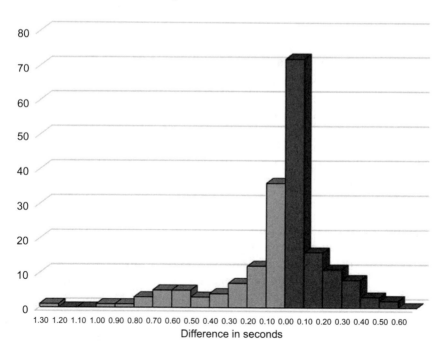

Figure 5.1 Differences between officer and suspect shot times. Note: Light grey bars denote the officer firing first and dark grey bars denote the suspect firing first. Wilson signed rank test p = .89.

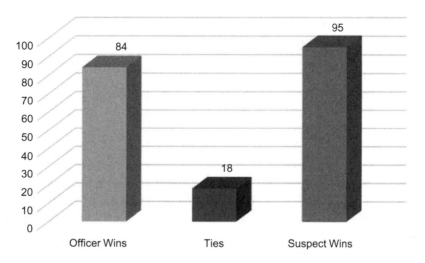

Figure 5.2 Suspect and officer wins.

Another way to look at this data is to examine the number of runs in which the suspect fired before the officer or vice versa. In 84 of the runs, the officer fired first (See Figure 5.2). The officer and suspect fired at precisely the same time (i.e., tied) in 18 runs. Further, in 95 runs, the suspect fired first. Taken together, these results clearly indicate that the first officer to enter the room cannot be expected to consistently fire before the suspect.

Accuracy. Accuracy data was available for all 207 runs completed by the 69 participants. The participants fired a total of 828 rounds at the entering officers. These shots hit the officers 373 times for a hit rate of 45%.

Figure 5.3 shows the number of hits on the first officer by condition. During the unknown entry, the first officer was hit an average of 1.94 times (SD = 1.08). During the hybrid entry, the first officer was hit an average of 1.28 times (SD = .84), and during the known entry, the first officer was hit an average of 1.10 times (SD = .93). The differences between conditions were large enough to conclude that entry type had a moderate effect on the number of shots that hit the first officer. More specifically, the first officer was hit more often in the unknown conditions than in the known and hybrid conditions.

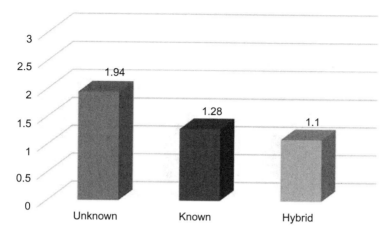

Figure 5.3 Hits on the first officer to enter by entry type. Note: $F_{(2,67)} = 15.91$, p = .000, $\eta2 = .20$. Significant post hoc means tests Unknown > Known and Hybrid.

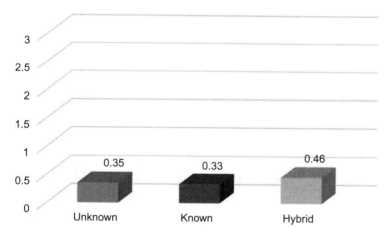

Figure 5.4 Hits on second officer by entry type. Note: $F_{(2,67)} = 1.23$, $p = .30$, $\eta^2 = .02$.

Figure 5.4 presents the number of hits on the second officer to enter the room. In the unknown entry condition, the second officer was hit an average of .35 times (SD = .59). The mean number of hits on the second officer in the hybrid condition was .33 (SD = .56), and the mean number of hits on the second officer in the known condition was .46 (SD = .61). These differences were not large enough to confidently conclude that hits on the second officer were affected by entry type.

Recall that one of the criticisms of the unknown entry is that the second officer has to travel behind the first officer and through the suspect's field

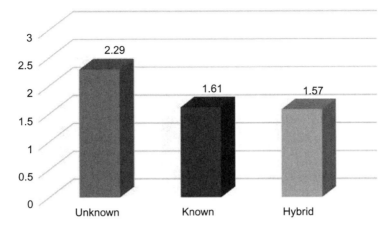

Figure 5.5 Combined hits on officers by entry type. Note: $F_{(2,67)} = 13.41$, $p = .000$, $\eta^2 = .15$. Significant post hoc means tests Unknown > Known and Hybrid.

of fire in order to get into firing position, and that this could expose the second officer to fire intended for the first officer. The second officer was hit while passing behind the first in 11 out of the 69 (or 16%) unknown entries.

Figure 5.5 presents the combined number of hits on the officers. The mean number of hits in the unknown conditions was 2.29 (SD = 1.02). The mean number of hits in the hybrid conditions was 1.61 (SD = .99), and in the known conditions, the mean was 1.57 (SD = 1.13). These differences were large enough to conclude that entry type had a moderate effect on the number of times that officers were hit. Specifically, officers were hit more in the unknown conditions than in the known and hybrid conditions.

5.1.3 Experiment 1 Discussion

These results indicate that the first officer to enter a room cannot consistently expect to shoot before the suspect. The results also clearly support the contention that lateral movement degrades the accuracy of suspects. Both in terms of total number of hits and hits on the first officer, the known and hybrid entries appear to be superior to the unknown entry. Additionally, the belief that the second officer can be hit while moving behind the first in the unknown entry was confirmed. In 16% of the unknown runs, rounds aimed at the first officer hit the second officer. Considering that the force-on-force round cannot penetrate the first officer's clothing or body, this number can reasonably be expected to be higher when dealing with actual firearms. We turn now to the impact of the entries on the accuracy of the first officer.

5.2 EXPERIMENT 2

Twenty-eight participants in an active shooter conference agreed to participate in the study. All of the participants were male, and the majority of participants (64%) were white. All but three of the participants were licensed police officers at the time of the study. The three unlicensed participants were members of the military. The average number of years of policing experience was 13.36 (SD = 6.56). The mean number of years of tactical (SWAT) police experience in the sample was 9.96 (SD = 7.41). All of the participants had participated in force-on-force training similar to what was done in this experiment.

5.2.1 Methodology

Participants were randomly paired with a partner and assigned to the role of first officer or second officer. This created 14 entry teams. Each team received approximately 20 minutes of training in the three entry types. This training included allowing each team to practice each entry several times. After the training, the participants were taken to one of two entry rooms. These rooms were essentially identical in layout and dimensions. Both were corner fed rooms that opened to the participant's right (that is, the door was located in one of the corners of the room, and as the participant faced the door, the blind corner was to the participant's right-hand side). In each room, an assistant playing the role of a hostile suspect was placed in the blind corner. This assistant's role was to begin firing as soon as the first officer entered the room in order to increase the stress on the officers. Each team of officers completed each of the entries according to a fully counterbalanced schedule. Each officer had three rounds to fire at the suspect. Following each entry, hits were assessed, the room was reset, the officers and suspect rearmed, and the next entry was executed. This process was repeated until each team had executed all three entries. Each of the entries was videotaped using a camera recording at 30 frames per second.

5.2.2 Results

In the unknown condition, the first officers scored a mean of 1.50 (SD = 1.09, see Figure 5.6) hits on the suspect. During the hybrid

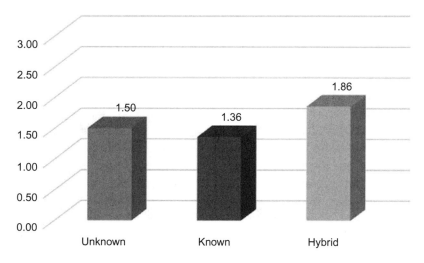

Figure 5.6 First officer hits on suspect by condition. Note: $F_{(2,26)} = 1.0$, $p = .38$, $\eta^2 = .07$.

condition, the first officers scored a mean of 1.86 (SD = 1.03) hits on the suspect, and in the known condition the first officers scored a mean of 1.36 (SD = .84) hits on the suspect. These differences were too small to confidently conclude that entry type affected officer accuracy.

5.2.3 Experiment 2 Discussion

The hit data from Experiment 2 suggested that if entry type affected the accuracy of the first officer entering the room, this effect was small. Because the sample size was relatively small, Experiment 3 sought to replicate this finding. Experiment 3 also examined the impact of the entries on the speed at which the second officer could engage the suspect.

5.3 EXPERIMENT 3

Ten members of a county-level SWAT team participated in the study. All of the participants were male, Caucasian, licensed police officers, and had participated in force-on-force training in the past. The mean age of the officers was 36.0 (SD = 5.03) years old. The participants had an average of 10.5 (SD = 3.92) years of policing experience and 5.20 (SD = 4.16) years of tactical experience.

5.3.1 Methodology

Participants were randomly paired with a partner. This created 5 entry teams. In this experiment, all participants played the role of first and, also, second officer in repeated trials. Each officer team completed six entries: three entries with one officer as the first officer, and then three with the other officer in the role of the first officer. The order of the entries was counterbalanced. Participants were given a brief review, lasting about 5 minutes, of the three entry types. Because all of the participants had previously practiced the entries during the course of their SWAT training, no practice runs were given. After the review, the participants were taken to the entry room. This was a corner fed room that opened to the participant's left (that is, the door was located in one of the corners of the room, and as the participant faced the door, the blind corner was to the participant's left-hand side). In each room, an assistant playing the role of a hostile suspect was placed in the blind corner. This assistant's role was to begin firing as soon as the first officer entered the room in order to increase the stress on the officers. The first officer had three rounds to fire at the suspect, and the second had a single round. Following each entry, hits were assessed, the room was reset, the officers and suspect rearmed, and the next entry was executed. This process was repeated until each team had executed all six entries. Each of the entries was videotaped using a camera recording at 30 frames per second.

Two coders evaluated the videos. The first coded all of the videos and the second coded 20% to provide a reliability check. Reliability was high. Two variables were coded. The first was the time at which the first officer entered the room. The second was the time at which the second officer fired.

5.3.2 Results

First officer accuracy. In the unknown condition, the first officers scored a mean of 1.80 (SD = .91, see Figure 5.7) hits on the suspect. In the hybrid condition, the first officers scored a mean of 2.10 (SD = .99) hits on the suspect, and in known condition the first officers scored a mean of 2.20 (SD = .78) hits on the suspect. These differences were not large enough to confidently conclude that entry type affected officer accuracy.

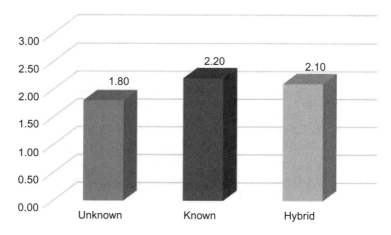

Figure 5.7 First officer hits on suspect by condition. Note: $F_{(2,18)} = .47$, $p = .47$, $\eta^2 = .05$.

Shot speed of second officer. Shot speed of the second officer was calculated as the time that elapsed from when the first officer crossed the threshold of the door until the second officer fired. In the unknown conditions, the second officer fired in an average of 1.61 seconds (SD = .12, see Figure 5.8) after the first officer entered the room. The mean time for the second officer to fire in the hybrid conditions was 1.31 seconds (SD = .14), and in the known conditions, the mean time to fire was 1.29 seconds (SD = .19). These differences suggested that entry type had a large impact on the shot speed of the second officer. The second officer was slower to fire in the unknown conditions than in the known and hybrid conditions.

5.3.3 Experiment 3 Discussion

When officers were completing the unknown entry, the second officer was significantly slower to fire than in the hybrid and known entries. This difference was only about .3 seconds; however, in an active gun battle, .3 seconds can be enough time for a suspect to fire several rounds at the first officer.

As in Experiment 2, the hit data from Experiment 3 suggested that if entry type affected the accuracy of the first officer entering the room, this effect was small. Discussions with members of the SWAT team suggested two issues that might keep the entries from affecting accuracy. The first suggestion was that, during a known entry into a

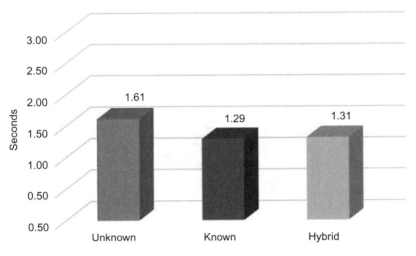

Figure 5.8 Second officer time to fire. Note: $F_{(2,18)} = 22.86$, $p = .000$, $\eta^2 = .71$. Significant post hoc means tests Unknown > Known and Hybrid.

left-hand opening room, it is easier for a right-handed shooter to compensate for the effects of the lateral movement than during the same entry into a right-hand opening room. Since most of our shooters were right-handed, this could explain the lack of difference in accuracy. This was not a particularly compelling explanation because the rooms opened to the right in Experiment 2. A second suggestion was that the first officer slowed his shots in order to make them more accurate during the known entry. This was a much more plausible explanation, as it is well accepted that there is a speed/accuracy tradeoff when shooting, with more speed resulting in less accuracy and vice versa. This belief is also supported by reaction time research (Simen et al., 2009).

To explore this contention, we assessed the time it took the first officer to fire his first shot. The mean time to fire for the first officer in the unknown entries was .64 seconds (SD = .16, see Figure 5.9). The mean time to fire for the first officer in the hybrid conditions was .70 (SD = .12), and in the known conditions, it was .77 (SD = .25). While these differences were moderate in size, they were not large enough to be confident that entry type affected the shot speed of the first officer due to a peculiarity in the structure of the data (see the note under Figure 5.9 for more details).

Given the completely post hoc and equivocal nature of this finding, Experiment 4 was conducted to assess the speed with which the first

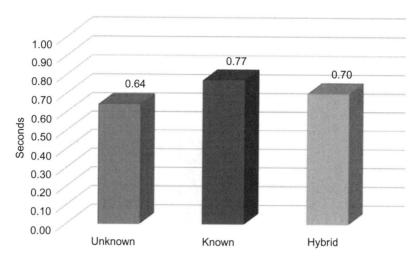

Figure 5.9 First officer time to fire by entry type. Note: $F_{(2,18)} = 3.79$, $p = .04$, $\eta^2 = .30$ — However, Mauchly's W, testing the sphericity assumption, was .41 ($p = .02$), suggesting that the assumption was violated. Corrections for this violation pushed the p of the F test above the conventional $p < .05$ level ($p = .07$ to .08 depending on the specific correction).

officer fired in an a priori manner and provide additional replication of the previous results.

5.4 EXPERIMENT 4

Fourteen members of a county-level SWAT team participated in the study.[1] All of the participants were male, licensed police officers, and had previously participated in force-on-force training. The majority of participants (78.6%) were Caucasian. The mean age was 37.0 (SD = 4.74) years. The average number of years of police experience was 12.32 (SD = 4.28), and the mean years of tactical experience was 6.36 (SD = 4.92).

5.4.1 Methodology

Participants were randomly paired with a partner. This created seven entry teams. Each officer team completed six entries; three entries with one officer as the first officer, and then three with the other officer in the role of the first officer. The order of the entries was counterbalanced. The rest of the procedure was almost identical to that used in

---

[1]Approximately one third of participants of this Experiment (4) also participated in Experiment 3. The experiments were conducted about 1 year apart. Exclusion of these repeat participants did not substantially affect the results.

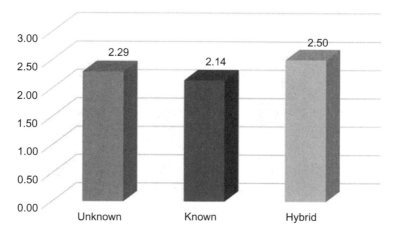

Figure 5.10 First officer hits on suspect by entry. Note: $F_{(2,26)} = 1.21$, $p = .32$, $\eta^2 = .08$.

Experiment 3, with the exception that a different right-hand opening room was used.

Coding was conducted in the same way as Experiment 3. Agreement on the variables was high.

5.4.2 Results

First officer accuracy. In the unknown conditions, the first officers scored a mean of 2.29 (SD = .91, see Figure 5.10) hits on the suspect. In the hybrid conditions, the first officers scored a mean of 2.50 (SD = .65) hits on the suspect, and in the known conditions the first officers scored a mean of 2.14 (SD = .54) hits on the suspect. This difference was again too small to confidently conclude that entry type had an effect on the accuracy of the first officer.

Shot speed of second officer. Shot speed of the second officer was calculated as the time that elapsed from when the first officer crossed the threshold of the door until the second officer fired. In the unknown conditions, the second officer fired in an average of 2.10 seconds (SD = .36, see Figure 5.11) after the first officer entered the room. The mean time to fire for the second officer in the hybrid conditions was 1.70 seconds (SD = .49), and in the known conditions, the mean time to fire was 1.63 seconds (SD = .36). These differences suggested the entry type had a large effect on the shot speed of the second officer. The second officer was slower to fire in the unknown conditions than in either the known or hybrid conditions.

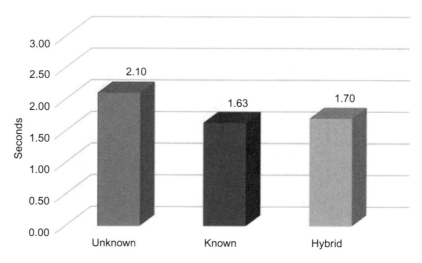

Figure 5.11 Second officer time to fire by entry. Note: $F_{(2,26)} = 12.68$, $p = .000$, $\eta^2 = .49$. *Post hoc means tests Unknown > Known and Hybrid.*

Shot speed of first officer. The shot speed of the first officer was calculated as the time that elapsed from when he crossed the threshold of the door until he fired the first shot. In the unknown conditions, the first officer took an average of .89 (SD = .27, see Figure 5.12) seconds to fire the first shot. The mean was .96 (SD = .31) seconds in the hybrid conditions, and 1.20 seconds (SD = .45) in the known conditions. These differences suggested that entry type had a moderate effect on the shot speed of the first officer. More specifically, the first officer was slower to fire in the known conditions than in the unknown and hybrid conditions.

5.4.3 Experiment 4 Discussion
Experiment 4 again failed to find a difference in accuracy large enough to rule out random error. If there is a difference, the difference is small. The results also revealed that perhaps the reason we failed to observe a decrease in the accuracy of the officers during the known entry was because the first officer was slowing down his speed of fire to make more accurate shots. The first officer was taking about .3 seconds longer to make his first shot in the known condition. This suggests that the officers knew that the shot was more difficult and slowed down accordingly. Experiment 4 also replicated results from Experiment 3 of

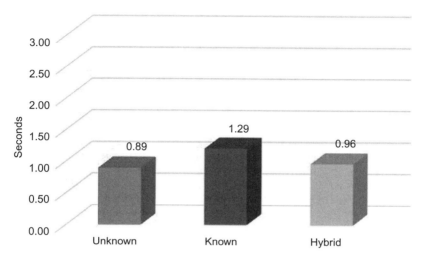

Figure 5.12 First officer time to fire. Note: $F_{(2,26)} = 6.69$, $p = .005$, $\eta^2 = .34$. Significant post hoc means tests Known > Hybrid and Unknown.

the time for the second officer to fire. The second officer took about .4 seconds longer to fire in the unknown condition than in the others.

5.5 OVERALL DISCUSSION

Experiment 1 examined the reaction times of suspects relative to the officer entries. We found that while the officers fired on average about .04 seconds faster than the suspects in our sample, this difference was not large enough to discount the possibility that the observed difference was the product of random error. Additionally, when we examined who shot first in each exchange, the suspects fired at the same time or before the officers in 57% of the encounters.

Experiment 1 also dealt with whether the different entries affected the accuracy of the suspects. Both of the entries that included lateral movement (hybrid and known) resulted in fewer hits on the police officers than the unknown entry. More specifically, the officers were hit with about .6 fewer rounds in the known and hybrid entries than in the unknown entry. As common sense would suggest, it appears that hitting a target that is moving laterally in relationship to the shooter is more difficult than shooting a target that is moving directly toward the shooter.

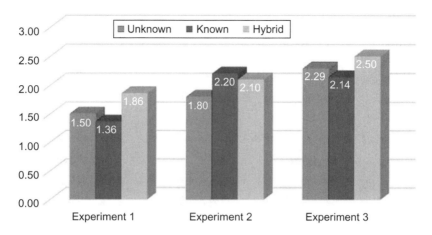

Figure 5.13 Comparison of first officer hits on suspects across experiments.

Experiments 2–4 addressed whether or not the entries affected the accuracy of the first officer to enter. Across all three experiments, we failed to find a significant difference by entry for the first officers and consistently observed small differences. These experiments all had small sample sizes, so it is possible that with a larger sample, a significant difference would have been found, but a few comments regarding this are warranted. First, in a large enough sample, it is a statistical certainty that any observed difference will be significant. This does not mean that the finding is meaningful. Again, the differences between conditions that we observed were quite small.

Second, the use of repeated measures designs in experiments is more efficient (powerful) than the use of independent groups designs because individual differences are controlled. Clearly, we had enough statistical power to detect the effects of the entries on our other measures.

Third, as can be seen in Figure 5.13, a consistent pattern of results was not observed. Often, the entry believed to be the most accurate (unknown) did not have a sample mean that was higher than one of the other conditions. The effect of the entries on accuracy, then, appears to be small, at best, if it exists at all. We did find, however, that the speed with which officers fired in the known entry was a little slower than in the other two entries. This suggests that the officers recognized that it was more difficult to fire accurately during the known entries and slowed their fire to increase their accuracy.

Table 5.1 Performance of the Entries on Outcome Measures				
Entry	Reduced Suspect Accuracy	1st Officer Accuracy	1st Officer Speed of Fire	2nd Officer Speed of Fire
Unknown		+	+	
Hybrid	+	+	+	+
Known	+	+		+

The speed with which the second officer engaged the suspect was assessed in Experiments 3 and 4. In both experiments, we found that the second officer was about one third of a second slower to fire in the unknown entries than in the other two. This makes intuitive sense in that the unknown entry is the only one that requires the second officer to move behind and past the first officer to establish a clear arc of fire. We also found that the second officer was occasionally hit by rounds intended for the first officer while the second officer passed behind the first.

The obvious question is: Which entry is superior? We have prepared Table 5.1 to help the reader assess this question. A plus indicates that a particular entry was the best in a particular category. If two or more techniques were better than another, but not significantly different from each other, they were both given a plus. If no technique was significantly better than another, all three were given pluses. As can be seen in Table 5.1, only the hybrid entry has pluses in every category, which suggests that it performed better than the others. It appears that the hybrid entry succeeds in combining the strengths of both the unknown and known entries while avoiding the weaknesses of both.

We are not arguing that the hybrid is the best entry for all situations. The type of entry that is used will be determined by the specifics of the situation. The positioning of furniture, for example, may preclude the use of some types of entries. Our research simply seeks to provide empirical data to inform practitioner's decisions.

We do believe that two general principles regarding entries can be derived from our data. First, lateral movement on the part of the entering officer reduces suspect accuracy. This movement causes the suspect to have to shift his or her shooting platform either to the left or right to accurately track the officer, and this is more difficult than tracking an officer who is moving directly toward or away from the suspect (Rayburn, 2004; Spaulding, 2010). If the lateral motion is too extreme, it may interfere with the officer's ability to shoot. In our research, this interference was manifested in slower firing times. Shallow lateral motion (i.e., motion that is 45 degrees or less to either side of the suspect) does not appear to affect the ability of officers to fire but still conveys the advantage of reduced suspect accuracy.

Second, if the second officer has to move behind the first to enter, the second officer will be slower to engage the suspect than if the second officer can move straight in. This may seem obvious and not particularly important, but it is. Our reaction time data showed that officers fired before the suspect in only 42% of their engagements. Even in the engagements where the officer "won," the officer was often only a few hundredths of a second faster than the suspect, suggesting that the suspect would still get at least one shot off at the officer in many of these exchanges. Granted, the suspect knew that the officers would be coming sometime after the scenario was called hot, but they did not know exactly when. Sometimes the officers would enter immediately when the scenario was called hot, sometimes they would delay for a few seconds, and sometimes they would wait a minute or more. Regardless of what the officers did, the suspect still fired at the same time or faster than the officer in the majority of these exchanges.

This is despite the fact that the decision to shoot for the entering officers was much easier than the decision would be in the real world. The officers knew there would be a suspect and that the suspect would be armed and hostile. They also knew that no one would be hurt and that disciplinary and/or legal actions would not follow the decision to shoot. These differences should have produced faster firing times for the officers than would be observed in the real world.

A large body of reaction time research supports the contention that the suspect will be able to fire before the officers because the officers must observe the suspect, detect that he or she is a threat, decide they need to shoot and that no innocent is in their arc of fire, and then shoot; whereas, the suspect can just see movement and shoot because he or she has already decided to shoot whoever enters. Our research, combined with the general reaction time research, strongly suggests that the suspect will fire before the first officer during many entries. This means that there is a high likelihood that the first officer will be shot immediately upon entry and emphasizes the importance of the second officer getting into firing position as soon as possible. Additionally, there is a chance that the second officer will be shot when moving behind the first officer if the second officer's entry path takes him that way. These findings further highlight the danger of conducting room entries.

Like all research, our experiments were not without limitations. While we tried to capture the basic dynamics of conducting room entries against hostile suspects, it is simply not possible to simulate the real danger faced by police officers on the street. As such, we suspect that our officers would experience substantially more stress when conducting actual room entries and that this stress might impair their performance. For example, the accuracy of our suspects and officers was substantially higher than is commonly observed in actual shootings (Alpert & Dunham, 1995; Fitzgerald & Bromley, 1998; White, 2006). As such, our results probably represent a best case scenario for actual officer performance. That being said, we tried to add some stress by having the suspects and officers actively shoot at each other with force-on-force rounds. These rounds mimic the sounds of actual gunfire and also sting when they hit. This type of training is generally considered to produce moderate levels of stress (Grossman & Christensen, 2008). Despite these limitations, we believe that we were able to produce information that is relevant to best practices. We turn now to our concluding thoughts.

CHAPTER 6

Conclusion

In the first part of this work, we examined the impact of using a dump or slice style entry on officer performance. We found that, compared to the slice conditions, officers took approximately twice as long to respond to a second gunman in the dump conditions. Once the officers in the dump conditions detected the second gunman in the room, they were almost 5 times more likely to violate the universal firearms safety rules and commit a priority of fire violation. The first officer also momentarily stalled in the doorway during 18% of the dump entries but never stalled during a slice entry. We did observe more instances of the officers in the slice entry shooting at the innocent suspect in the room, but this difference was not large enough to be confident that it was not the product of chance assignment error. Taken together, we argued that the data suggested that the slice was a better entry style than the dump to teach patrol officers.

In the second section of this book, we addressed the impact that variations in the slice entry had on officer performance. These differences primarily have to do with the direction that the first officer goes when he or she enters a room. We found several things. First, the officers cannot expect to fire before the suspect when conducting a room entry. Second, if the first officer to enter moves laterally in relationship to the suspect, the suspect's accuracy will be reduced. This lateral movement did not reduce the accuracy of the officer's fire on the suspect, but when the lateral movement was approximately 90 degrees to the suspect, the speed at which the officer fired was reduced. This did not happen when the angle was approximately 45 degrees. Third, entries that required the second officer to move behind and past the first officer in order to fire at the suspect delayed the speed with which the second officer could engage the suspect. Fourth, the second officer was occasionally hit by fire intended for the first officer while passing behind the first officer. Taken together, these findings supported the use of the hybrid entry. The hybrid entry involves the first officer entering at about a 45-degree angle to the blind corner and the second officer moving directly toward the blind corner.

We have two sets of concluding comments for our readers. One is targeted at police officers and one at academics. We begin with our comments for police officers.

6.1 TO POLICE OFFICERS

For years, tactical police officers have debated the merits and faults of commonly used entry styles and techniques. We have heard some officers suggest that the tactics in use at particular police departments are the result of who out-argued, out-ranked, or out-experienced the other side. In others, officers have suggested that the tactics taught at a particular department are simply the product of what the officers before them were doing. This is unfortunate, because we believe that you do an important job and deserve to have the best information possible.

In this book, we set out to apply both scientific theory and empirical testing to assess commonly used room entry styles and techniques. We do not claim any tactical experience. Neither of us has ever been a police officer, much less a tactical officer. On one hand, this was a disadvantage; we did not know much about tactical policing at the start of this project. To fill our knowledge voids, we have read as much as we could, talked to hundreds of police officers, observed thousands of hours of training, and participated in training sessions where possible. On the other hand, this lack of knowledge may have been beneficial in that we didn't have a "horse in the race," so to speak. Hopefully, this helped us to maintain our objectivity.

Our examination was focused on patrol officers, but we think that the work also has implications for tactical teams. Our findings and the relevant theories clearly support the use of the hasty slice style combined with the hybrid entry technique. Based upon our current data, we would recommend these as best practices for training patrol officers.

Science, however, is never complete. It never definitively proves something; rather, science represents the best knowledge that we currently possess on a topic. One of the best features of science is that it provides a system for challenging (and, where necessary, replacing) existing beliefs. Many of you will find flaws in our experiments and disagree with our conclusions. We welcome this and encourage you to contact us. As we said, we do not have a horse in this race. We simply seek to provide the best information that we can to inform best practices and improve police officer performance.

6.2 TO ACADEMICS

We hope that this work will generate interest in assessing police tactics. As you can see from our literature reviews, there is little in the criminology/criminal justice literature to draw upon as a base. We as academics have done little to improve best practices in this area but tend to be quick to condemn police when we think they have made tactical mistakes (e.g., shooting a person who was holding a phone). The use of poor tactics can cost the lives not only of police officers, but also innocent citizens.

While officers are sometimes resistant to examination by outsiders, we have found that they are quite receptive and appreciative once they discover that you are there to help and not condemn. Officers also tend to be very practical. They want things that work or work better. If you can provide either, you will be appreciated and just might save some lives (police officer or civilian). Surely, that is worth the effort.

REFERENCES

Alpert, G. P., & Dunham, R. G. (1995). *Police use of deadly force: A statistic analysis of the Metro-Dade Police Department*. Washington, DC: Police Executive Research Forum.

Ando, S., Kida, N., & Oda, S. (2002). Practice effects on reaction time for peripheral and central visual fields. *Perceptual and Motor Skills*, *95*(3), 747–751.

Ando, S., Kida, N., & Oda, S. (2004). Retention of practice effects on simple reaction time for peripheral and central visual fields 1. *Perceptual and Motor Skills*, *98*(3), 897–900.

Artwohl, A., & Christensen, L. W. (1997). *Deadly force encounters: What cops need to know to mentally and physically prepare for and survive a gunfight*. Boulder, CO: Paladin Press.

Beyler, C. L. (2009). *Analysis of the fire investigation methods and procedures used in the criminal arson cases against Ernest Ray Willis and Cameron Todd Willingham*. Hughes Associates.

Bittner, E. (1970). *The functions of the police in modern society*. New York, NY: Aronson.

Blair, J. P., Levine, T. R., Reimer, T., & McCluskey, J. D. (2012). The gap between reality and research: Another look at detecting deception in field settings. *Policing: An International Journal of Police Strategies and Management*, *35*, 723–740.

Blair, J. P., Nichols, T., Burns, D., & Curnutt, J. R. (2013). *Active shooter events and response*. Baco Raton, FL: CRC Press Llc.

Blair, J. P., Pollock, J., Montague, D., Nichols, T., Curnutt, J., & Burns, D. (2011). Reasonableness and reaction time. *Police Quarterly*, *14*(4), 323–343.

Boyd, J. R. (1995). The essence of winning and losing. Retrieved from <http://www.namepa.net/events5thAnniv/SUNY_Video.pdf> on 19/08/13.

Braga, A. A., Papachristos, A. V., & Hureau, D. M. (2012). The effects of hot spots policing on crime: An updated systematic review and meta-analysis. Justice Quarterly, *(ahead-of-print)* 1–31.

Bureau of Justice Statistics (BJS) (2008). *Police-public contact survey*. Washington D.C.: Office of Justice Programs. Office of Justice Programs, Bureau of Justice Statistics.

Campbell, J. H. (1992). *A comparative analysis of the effects of post-shooting trauma on the special agents of the Federal Bureau of Investigation*. Unpublished Ph.D. Dissertation. Department of Educational Administration, Michigan State University.

Edwards, H., & Gotsonis, C. (2009). Strengthening forensic science in the United States: A path forward. *Statement before the United State Senate Committee on the Judiciary*.

Federal Bureau of Investigation (FBI). (2011). *Law enforcement officers killed and assaulted*. Retrieved from <http://www.fbi.gov/about-us/cjis/ucr/leoka/2011> on 19/08/13.

Fitzgerald, S. C., & Bromley, M. L. (1998). Surviving deadly force encounters: A case study. *Journal of Police and Criminal Psychology*, *13*, 25–35.

Force Science Institute. (n.d.). *Force Science News #215: Badge placement affects survival odds for plainclothes cops*. Retrieved 17 April 2013, from <www.forcescience.org/fsnews/215.html>.

Force Science Institute. (n.d.). *Force Science News #216: Readers' opinions, experiences, finding on blue-on-blue tragedies*. Retrieved 17 April 2013, from <www.forcescience.org/fsnews/216.html>.

Friedland, N., & Keinan, G. (1992). Training effective performance in stressful situations: Three approaches and implications for combat training. *Military Psychology*, *4*, 157–174.

Geller, W., & Scott, M. (1992). *Deadly force: What we know*. Washington, DC: Police Executive Research Forum.

Gigerenzer, G. (2008). *Rationality for mortals: How people cope with uncertainty*. Oxford: Oxford University Press.

Grossman, D., & Christensen, L. W. (2008). *On combat: The psychology and physiology of deadly conflict in war and in peace* (3rd ed.). Milstadt, IL: Warrior Science Publications.

Hickman, M. J., Piquero, A. R., & Garner, J. H. (2008). Toward a national estimate of police use of nonlethal force. *Criminology and Public Policy, 7*, 563–604.

Horvath, F., & Donahue, M. (1982). *Deadly force: An analysis of shootings by police in Michigan, 1976–1981*. East Lansing: Michigan State University.

Just, M. A., & Carpenter, P. A. (1976). Eye fixations and cognitive processes. *Cognitive Psychology, 8*, 441–480.

Kahneman, D. (2011). *Thinking fast: Thinking slow*. New York: Farrar, Straus, and Giroux.

Kahneman, D., & Klein, G. (2009). Conditions for intuitive expertise: A failure to disagree. *American Psychologist, 64*, 515–526.

Klinger, D., & Brunson, R. (2009). Police officers' perceptual distortions during lethal force situations: Informing the reasonableness standard. *Criminology and Public Policy, 8*(1), 117–140.

Lewinski, B., & Hudson, B. (2003). The impact of visual complexity, decision making and anticipation: The Temple study, experiments 3 and 5. *The Police Marksman, 28*(6), 24–27.

Luce, R. D. (1986). *Response times: Their role in inferring elementary mental organization* (Vol. 8). Oxford University Press.

Morrison, G. B., & Cooper, J. (1991). *The modern technique of the pistol*. Paulden, AZ: Gunsite Press.

New York State Task Force on Police-on-Police Shootings. (2010). *Reducing inherent danger: Report of the Task Force on Police-on-Police Shootings* (Full Report and Appendixes). New York, NY: NCJRS Abstracts.

ODMP. (2010, May 3). *Police Officer Brian Eric Huff*. Retrieved July 23, 2013, from Officer Down Memorial Page: <http://www.odmp.org/officer/20394-police-officer-brian-eric-huff>.

Pate, A., & Hamilton, E. E. (1991). *The big six: Policing America's largest cities*. Washington, DC: Police Foundation.

Pierce, G., Spaar, S., & Briggs, L. (1988). *The character of police work: Strategic and tactical implications*. Boston, MA: Center for Applied Social Research, Northeastern University.

Rayburn, M. (2004, January 21). *Shooting on the move: Using your instincts*. Retrieved 18 August 2013, from PoliceOne: <http://www.policeone.com/columnists/PoliceMagazine/articles/77165-Shooting-on-the-move-using-your-instincts/>.

Reppetto, T. (1976). Crime prevention and the displacement phenomenon. *Crime & Delinquency, 22*, 166–177.

Rieskamp, J., & Reimer, T. (2007). Ecological rationality. In R. F. Baumeister, & K. D. Vohs (Eds.), *Encyclopedia of social psychology* (pp. 273–275). Thousand Oaks, CA: Sage.

Rogers, M. W., Johnson, M. E., Martinez, K. M., Mille, M. L., & Hedman, L. D. (2003). Step training improves the speed of voluntary step initiation in aging. *The Journals of Gerontology Series A: Biological Sciences and Medical Sciences, 58*(1), M46–M51.

Ruch, T. C. (1965). Vision. In T. C. Ruch, & H. D. Patton (Eds.), *Physiology and biophysics*. Philadelphia: Saunders.

Sherman, L. (1998). *Evidence-based policing. Ideas in American policing*. Washington, DC: Police Foundation. July.

Sherman, L., Farrington, D., Welsh, B., & MacKenzie, D. (Eds.), (2002). *Evidence-based crime prevention.* New York: Routledge.

Sherman, L., Gartin, P., & Buerger, M. (1989). Hot spots of predatory crime: Routine activities and the criminology of place. *Criminology, 27,* 27−56.

Simen, P. D., Contreras, D., Buck, C., Hu, P., Holmes, P., & Cohen, J. D. (2009). Reward rate optimization in two-alternative decision making: Empirical tests of theoretical predictions. *Journal of Experimental Psychology: Human Perception and Performance, 35,* 1865−1898.

Simon, H. A. (1956). Rational choice and the structure of the environment. *Psychological Review, 63,* 129−138.

Sokolov, E. N., Spinks, J. A., Näätänen, R., & Lyytinen, H. (2002). *The orienting response in information processing.* Lawrence Erlbaum Associates Publishers.

Solomon, R. M., & Horn, J. H. (1986). Post-shooting traumatic reactions: A pilot study. In J. T. Reese, & H. A. Goldstein (Eds.), *Psychological services for law enforcement officers.* Washington, D.C.: U.S. Government Printing Office.

Spaulding, D. (2010, June 1). *Shooting while moving: This technique must be taught, learned & mastered.* Retrieved 18 August 2013, from LawOfficer Police & Law Enforcement: <http://www.lawofficer.com/article/training/shooting-while-moving>.

Ungerleider, L. G., & Mishkin, M. (1982). Two cortical visual systems. In D. J. Ingle, M. A. Goodale, & R. J. W. Mansfield (Eds.), *Analysis of visual behavior* (pp. 549−586). Boston: MIT Press.

Visser, I., Raijmakers, M. E., & Molenaar, P. C. (2007). Characterizing sequence knowledge using online measures and hidden Markov models. *Memory & Cognition, 35*(6), 1502−1517.

Weisburd, D., Ajzenstadt, M., Mazerolle, L., Wilson, D. B., Maxwell, C., & Schnurr, R. (Eds.), (2005). *Editors' introduction.* In: *Journal of Experimental Criminology* 1, 1−8.

Weisburd, D., Maher, L., & Sherman, L. (1992). *Contrasting crime general and crime specific theory: The case of hot spots of crime. Advances in criminological theory* (vol. 4, pp. 45−69). New Brunswick, NJ: Transaction Press.

Welford, A. T. (1980). Choice reaction time: Basic concepts. In A. T. Welford (Ed.), *Reaction times* (pp. 73−128). New York: Academic Press.

White, M. (2006). Hitting the target (or not): Comparing characteristics of fatal, injurious, and noninjurious police shootings. *Police Quarterly, 9,* 303−330.

Williams, A., Davids, K., & Williams, J. (2000). *Visual perception & action in sport.* New York, NY: Routledge.

Test ?'s   IED's Mod 7

- Ammo - medical (loaded into mags)
- Radio fw will not set off bomb - Very rare
  don't stand over IED while using RFW.
- Angles & Air gaps

gles and air gaps - IED's

ow Sticks

robe Lights (Home depot)

ms cover 15ft

ms go it rolls into Your Team

ol of opportunity - BFR - Trash can

edge - Full frontal coverage

not Touch IED